# Story-Driven
# Employer
# Branding

# Story-Driven Employer Branding

*Introducing*
*The Magnetic Employer Branding Method™:*
*Matching Minds with Mission Through*
*Business Storytelling*

SUSANNA RANTANEN

**Publisher**
Employer Branding Agency Emine Oy Ltd
Helsinki, Finland

ISBN: 979-8-89694-073-9 (Paperback)
ISBN: 979-8-89694-074-6 (Hardcover)
ISBN: 979-8-89694-072-2 (Ebook)

**First Edition, 2025**
This book is a work of non-fiction. While every effort has been made to ensure the accuracy of the information presented herein, the author and publisher assume no responsibility for errors, inaccuracies, or omissions.

**Disclaimer**
This book is intended for informational and educational purposes only. Any numbers provided are theoretical or used solely as examples. The author and publisher accept no responsibility for any actions you take or do not take as a result of reading this book. No liability is assumed for any damages, losses, or negative consequences to any person or organization arising from action or inaction based on the information contained herein. References to websites, tools, or external resources are provided for informational purposes only. The author and publisher are not responsible for the content, availability, or accuracy of these resources. Websites mentioned may change, move, or become obsolete over time.

**Cover Image by:** William Oesch

# GET YOUR FREE GIFT

Claim your exclusive **Employer Brand Content Plan Trello Board**—the perfect tool to kickstart your journey in creating **Magnetic Employer Brand content**.

This ready-to-use Trello board is a light version of the tailored content plan template we provide to our clients as part of designing and implementing their story-driven employer brand using the **Magnetic Employer Branding Method™**.

It includes four proven employer brand content idea types and generative AI prompts to help you brainstorm content ideas for each type.

Simply copy the board, customize it to fit your company's goals, and start crafting content that truly resonates with your audience.

It's time to show the world what makes your company magnetic!

Get your copy by visiting: www.emine.fi/sdeb-freegift

For my husband and business partner, Leo. You give me everything a girl needs: daily hugs and morning dances, love, humor, care, a partner in crime, and a delicious meal every day.

For our son, Kasper. Everything I do, I do it for you. I love you more than the width and the volume of the Universe.

My global employer branding community who has kept me going all these years through ups and downs with your supportive feedback, encouragement, and attention. Your words have mattered. You matter.

# CONTENTS

# FOREWORD BY
# THE AUTHOR

..............................................................................

This book is not about crafting recruitment campaigns on social media. That book could have been written back in 2011, when I introduced a novel, content-based recruitment marketing method for social media that quickly made our family business a go-to partner for fast-growing, modern tech entrepreneurs. It also positioned us as Finland's first employer branding and recruitment marketing agency. Today, social media campaigns are a commodity—a tactical tool that, while useful, will not provide you with sustainable employer brand value. Nor will they address one of the biggest strategic challenges of modern organizations: talent retention.

Instead, this book is about a paradigm shift in employer branding—a complete transformation of how businesses think about, approach, and execute this vital function. What follows is a science-based employer brand marketing methodology that uses business storytelling and persuasive communication to connect talent minds with your company's mission.

The Magnetic Employer Branding Method™ isn't just a framework; it's a mindset shift. It will change the way you think, talk, and act—not just about employer branding, but about your entire organization, your people, and your business.

My journey to this methodology began in HR, where I spent over a decade immersed in the challenges and opportunities of growth companies. Growth demands talent, and talent demands trust, inspiration, and connection. I learned firsthand the pain of making miracles with tiny budgets and the power of aligning leadership, strategy, and communication to create impact. This methodology was born out of those experiences—designed to equip you with the tools to win over your stakeholders, optimize resources, and deliver measurable results. It speaks the language of the C-suite while empowering HR and marketing professionals to take the reins of employer branding with confidence.

This book is for those of you who are tired of random acts of marketing and wasted resources. It's for those who are ready to shift from tactical noise to a strategic, systematic approach that creates sustainable solutions to talent attraction and retention. If your vision is to see your business and your people thrive together, this book will guide and inspire you to tame these challenges with precision and purpose.

It doesn't matter if you're the one leading employer branding efforts in your organization or someone who recognizes the need for change and wants to rally the troops. This book will empower you to spark transformation, inspire your Magnetic Employer Branding team, and champion a new era of employer branding that doesn't just attract talent but inspires loyalty and drives business growth. Because at its core, a Magnetic Employer is an empathetic guide— an authority that draws in not only top talent but also stakeholders and customers.

And who wouldn't want to invest in or buy from a company known for its inspired, committed, and motivated workforce delivering on their promises with joy?

To get the most out of this book, I encourage you to do three things:

1. **Digest the methodology:** Understand The Magnetic Employer Branding Method™ and embrace the fundamental shift in perspective: The talent is the hero, and you (as the employer) are their trusted guide to better work and life.

2. **Audit your communication:** Assess your internal and external messaging. Is it focused on your company's needs, or does it show how you, as an employer, can help talent achieve the life they desire?

3. **Personify your organization:** Imagine your company culture and values as the personality of your organization—an "organization person" your current and future employees are compelled to follow, trust, and learn from.

When you implement this methodology, your employer branding will transform into meaningful conversations and communications that build trust, loyalty, and lasting connections between your organization and your people.

Writing this book has been one of the most challenging yet rewarding journeys of my career. I hope you find this methodology as inspiring and transformative as I have in developing it. May it guide you to create a workplace where people are not only proud to belong but also driven to achieve extraordinary things together.

Yours truly,

Susanna

*"Storytelling is by far the most underrated skill in business."*

GARY VAYNERCHUK

# INTRODUCTION

......................................................................................................................

# Business Storytelling to Match Minds with Mission

In a world where attention spans are shrinking but expectations are soaring, the ability to tell a story isn't just nice to have—it's the key to standing out. And yet, most businesses overlook storytelling when it comes to one of their most critical assets: their employer brand.

Here's the reality: Talented people don't join companies; they join futures they believe in. They're not just evaluating your salary packages or benefits—they're assessing the culture you've built, the values you uphold, and the vision you offer for their growth. Today's candidates are driven by purpose, potential, and progress, not just paychecks. And the same goes for the people already on your team. If they can't find value in what you stand for and where you're headed, they'll disengage—and eventually leave.

That's where The Magnetic Employer Branding Method™ comes in. This isn't just another framework for employer branding; it's a system that uses the timeless power of storytelling to match the aspirations of today's talent with the mission of your organization. Through five core principles, this method empowers employers to step into the role of a trusted guide, shaping a narrative that inspires talent to see themselves as the hero in your story. By the end of this book, you'll have the tools to craft a brand story that doesn't just attract talent but builds sustainable affinity—internally and externally.

This methodology is for leaders who know their people are the true competitive edge. Whether you're an HR leader, marketing expert, or CEO, this book will show you how to integrate storytelling into every corner of your employer brand, from defining your culture to measuring its ROI. Let's dive into the art and science of turning your business story into your greatest talent magnet.

## The Five Key Principles

Having set the stage for how The Magnetic Employer Branding Method™ leverages storytelling to attract and retain top talent, let's dive into its backbone: the Five Key Principles. These principles aren't just theoretical—they are practical, actionable steps that will transform how you connect with the people who can drive your organization forward. Each principle is rooted in the science of storytelling and persuasion, ensuring your employer brand becomes magnetic to the right audience.

### #1 The Talent is the Hero

Every great story revolves around a hero—a character facing challenges and searching for a guide to help them overcome obstacles and achieve a brighter future. In employer branding, the talent is the hero, not your company. This is the cornerstone of magnetic storytelling.

Here's why this works: According to the science of persuasion, when you decrease your power, you increase your influence. By addressing the struggles, aspirations, and pain points of your target audience, you create trust and genuine connection. When you show that you understand their journey and can offer a way forward—a career path that adds meaning and value to their lives—you become their guide, the partner they need to succeed.

Magnetic Employer Branding isn't about bragging; it's about positioning your organization as the catalyst for their success. When you make it about them—their ambitions, their growth, their story—you earn not just attention, but loyalty and advocacy. This idea extends beyond attraction—it transforms retention. Employees who see themselves as the heroes of your organizational story are more likely to stay, grow, and contribute.

## #2 The Employer is the Trusted Guide

What's a hero without a guide? Think of Yoda, Dumbledore, or Haymitch—they're the characters who mentor the hero, offering wisdom, empathy, and a plan for success. In your employer brand story, you are the guide. Your role is to provide the insight, tools, and opportunities that help talent achieve their goals.

Why is this so effective? Stories are the brain's favorite way to process information. Neuroscience tells us that stories are like oxygen for our minds—they clarify complex ideas, inspire action, and stick with us long after the facts are forgotten. As the employer, you are the "best supporting actor," empowering your people to take the lead and thrive.

Think of your favorite movie. The main character begins in crisis—facing challenges they can't solve alone. It's the guide's empathy, authority, and wisdom that help the hero navigate the journey and emerge victorious. This is exactly how your employer brand should function. Position yourself as the trusted guide, and talent will see you as the employer who empowers them to build the life and career they desire.

## #3 Key Story Themes, Not EVPs

Forget about those rigid employer value propositions (EVPs) that so many organizations cling to. They often lead to stagnant messaging that fails to resonate. Instead, focus on Key Story Themes—dynamic, storytelling-driven frameworks that guide your employer branding communication.

Key Story Themes are the lifeblood of organic and ongoing content creation. They shift your mindset from a "one-and-done" EVP project to a continuous storytelling process. These themes reflect your desired employer brand perceptions and are designed from two perspectives: your role as the guide and the talent's role as the hero.

By centering your communication around these themes, you create a consistent and compelling narrative that differentiates your brand. Whether you already have EVPs or not, Key Story Themes give you the structure to translate values and pillars into actionable, authentic storytelling that keeps your brand alive in the minds of your audience.

## #4 Employer Branding is an Ongoing Process

Employer branding is not a campaign. Campaigns are short term; branding is forever. Yet, many organizations still treat employer branding as a box to check during recruiting or as a flashy awareness campaign.

The truth is, employer branding is a consistent communication process, built on trust and engagement over time. Campaigns can grab attention, but what happens next? Without sustained communication, the momentum fades, and so does your relevance in the talent market.

With The Magnetic Employer Branding Method™, you'll move beyond "burst campaigns" and into a long-term strategy that consistently engages passive and active talent. It's this ongoing dialogue—not sporadic marketing efforts— that builds a brand people trust and want to connect with.

## #5 Data-Driven Marketing Keeps You on Track

Finally, the fifth principle ensures your efforts deliver tangible results: data-driven marketing. Without clear metrics and goals, even the best storytelling can lose its way.

This principle is about tying everything back to measurable outcomes—whether it is brand affinity, improving employee engagement and satisfaction rates, talent retention, or your employees' impact on customer experiences and satisfaction. Unlike traditional campaigns that burn through budgets, often with little accountability, a data-driven approach allows you to track, refine, and amplify what works. This ensures your employer branding not only resonates but also rewards your organization with real, measurable value.

Together, these five principles form the cornerstones of The Magnetic Employer Branding Method™—a system that redefines how organizations communicate, attract, and retain top talent. They provide a clear road map for creating a brand story that positions you as the trusted guide and your talent as the hero, setting the stage for the chapters to come.

## Who is This Methodology Designed For?

Let's be clear: This book isn't for everyone, and this methodology isn't a one-size-fits-all solution—it's for companies navigating the unique challenges of today's talent-driven economy. It's for the doers and dreamers who know that the way we communicate with talent is broken—and are ready to fix it.

Are you an HR leader struggling to get buy-in for employer branding initiatives? A talent acquisition expert tired of seeing great candidates slip away? A marketing professional tasked with employer branding but unsure where to start? Or perhaps you're a founder, co-founder, CEO or other business leader who knows your people and your combined expertise is your competitive advantage but you haven't figured out yet how to show it to the world.

Does your organization face any of these challenges?

- You're a fast-scaling company where growth depends on converting knowledge into revenue.
- Your business is undergoing a transformation that's shaking up your culture, ways of working, and people.

- You're scaling through mergers and acquisitions, trying to unify cultures while driving results.
- You're caught in the war for talent and need a standout employer brand to reposition yourself as a true Talent Magnet.

If you found yourself nodding to any of these, this methodology can offer the clarity, structure, and impact you've been searching for. While any organization can benefit from a systematic employer branding process, the biggest returns on investment often come to knowledge-driven companies struggling with talent shortages.

The Magnetic Employer Branding Method™ combines the art of storytelling with the science of persuasion to help you craft a brand that resonates, inspires, and converts. By the end of this book, you'll not only know what to do, but you'll have the tools, insights, and frameworks to actually do it—and see measurable results.

## Why it Works Specifically for Fast-Growth Companies

Fast-scaling businesses face unique challenges: rapid cultural shifts, employee uncertainty, and resistance to change. Leadership and internal communications often struggle to keep up, creating a fog of confusion about what success looks like and how daily work contributes to bigger goals. The Magnetic Employer Branding Method™ bridges this gap.

By connecting your strategic goals—your mission, customer promise, and desired market position—with the culture, values, and daily operations of your business, this methodology makes the purpose of your employees' work crystal clear. It transforms your internal story into a compelling external narrative, aligning change communication with employer branding to create a seamless, ongoing process.

Here's the magic: The science of storytelling and persuasion turns your company's transformation—whether it's chaos, growth, or reinvention—into a captivating "documentary" that resonates with your target audience. By sharing this story authentically through social media and content marketing, you attract talent who see themselves as part of your journey. This transparency not only builds trust but also filters in candidates who thrive in your dynamic environment and filters out those who prefer slower, more predictable workplaces—reducing costly hiring mistakes.

## Authenticity and Data-Driven Success

What sets this methodology apart? It's rooted in authenticity and driven by data. Unlike traditional employer branding, which often lacks measurable goals, The Magnetic Employer Branding Method™ focuses on aligning your brand with your real culture, people, and operations. Your organization's magnetism comes from your unique DNA—how your people lead, communicate, collaborate, and innovate. By highlighting these authentic elements, you create a brand story that stands out, not because it's flashy, but because it's real.

And let's talk about data. One of the most exciting aspects of this methodology is its measurable nature. We introduce clear goals, KPIs, and analytics, empowering you to track progress and prove ROI. If you're results driven like me, you'll love the satisfaction of seeing your employer branding strategy come to life on a beautifully crafted dashboard. Watching our clients light up as they connect with the data and realize the impact of their efforts has been the cherry on top for me!

This methodology started as a solution for fast-scaling tech companies, but as digital transformation reshapes every industry, it's now a lifeline for businesses of all types facing change, competition, or talent shortages. Whether you're building a high-growth team, navigating organizational chaos, or simply looking for a better way to engage and attract talent, The Magnetic Employer Branding Method™ offers a proven path forward.

## The Power of Business Storytelling

We've explored who this methodology is for, but what makes it truly unique? The answer lies in its foundation: the sciences of storytelling and persuasion, deeply rooted in human behavior. Storytelling isn't just an art—it's a science. It taps into the way our brains are wired to process information, build connections, and make decisions.

Business storytelling is at the heart of this methodology. It's the practice of using narrative techniques to communicate your company's mission, values, and purpose in a way that resonates emotionally with your audience. Instead of simply listing facts or pitching achievements, storytelling reframes your business as a relatable character—or more often, a guide—in a narrative where the employee, customer, or stakeholder is the hero.

Why does this work? Because our brains are biologically programmed to seek and respond to stories. It's how humans have made sense of the world for centuries, from oral traditions and epic poems to modern TikToks, Instagram Reels, and YouTube vlogs. Stories create order out of chaos, transforming information into something memorable, compelling, and actionable. This is exactly why storytelling has been a constant in human culture—and why it's such an untapped goldmine in employer branding.

## The Brain and Storytelling: A Match Made for Connection

What fascinates me most about storytelling is the science behind it. The way our brains respond to stories isn't learned; it's instinctive. Neuroeconomist Dr. Paul J. Zak explains this beautifully: "Stories effectively transmit important information and values from one individual or community to the next. Personal and emotionally compelling stories engage more of the brain and are better remembered than simply stating a set of facts."

Think about it. When faced with a new problem or situation, your brain automatically searches for similar patterns or experiences to make sense of what's happening. This innate response to stories is what makes them so powerful—and why they're such an effective tool in employer branding.

Stories bypass the analytical part of our brain, speaking directly to the emotional core where trust, loyalty, and connection are formed.

This book will show you how to use business storytelling to turn your employer brand into a narrative that creates meaningful conversations with your current and future employees. When your audience can see themselves in your story—feel their struggles acknowledged and their dreams supported—they're more likely to connect, engage, and ultimately become part of your journey.

## *What Makes a Great Story?*

Is it just an exciting plot or relatable characters? Not quite. A great story doesn't have to be elaborate or fictional—it simply needs to resonate emotionally and deliver a clear message. In the context of employer branding, a powerful story isn't about what your organization does or what you've achieved. It's about how your organization uses its experiences, empathy, and authority to help others succeed.

This is the core of a Hero's Career Story™, one of the first storytelling techniques I designed for HR marketing. Traditional "career stories" often read like bland resumes. But by reimagining them as authentic, emotionally compelling narratives, we created mini biographies that positioned employees as heroes and the employer as their guide. A Hero's Career Story™ frames an employee's journey as one of overcoming challenges and discovering opportunities with the employer's support. These stories not only showcase what the employer offers but also invite the reader to imagine their own transformation—what their career and life might look like if they joined this organization.

The results? Transformative. These stories resonated deeply with target talent segments, building trust, inspiring action, and creating lasting impressions of the employer brand. If you'd like to explore this approach further, I've included additional resources at the end of this book.

## *Storytelling as a Strategic Asset*

What makes storytelling so invaluable in employer branding is its ability to humanize your organization while strategically positioning your brand. Through storytelling, you can connect your business transformation, culture, and goals to the real-life experiences of employees, creating a cohesive narrative that builds loyalty internally and intrigues externally.

As we navigate the chapters ahead, you'll discover how to incorporate storytelling at every stage of your employer branding journey. From crafting narratives that position talent as heroes to using data to validate your impact, storytelling will become not just a tool, but the language your brand speaks fluently.

Let's unlock the power of storytelling and transform your employer brand into a narrative that captivates, connects, and converts.

# THE FOUNDATION OF MAGNETIC EMPLOYER BRANDING

## CHAPTER 1

# Your Company Culture is the Personality of Your Organization

*"Every organization has a culture. The question is, does it have the culture it needs to succeed?"*

FRANCES FREI

L et's talk about company culture—the topic every workplace loves to discuss, but few truly understand. Culture is not just about team lunches, employee perks, or Friday yoga sessions. While these may reflect aspects of your culture, they're not the engine that drives it. In fact, many organizations mistakenly confuse culture with morale boosters or engagement tools, leaving the true potential of culture untapped.

At its core, company culture is the personality of your organization—the "how" of everything you do. It's the unspoken system that governs decisions, interactions, and outcomes. And here's the kicker: Whether you've consciously built it or not, your company already has a culture. The question is whether it's the one you need to achieve your goals.

## The Strategic Role of Culture

Culture isn't just a "nice to have." It's a strategic lever for business success. Your culture should act as the operating system of your organization, aligning the behavior of your people with your strategic goals. Without this alignment, even the best business strategies fall flat. Why? Because it's your people who execute the strategy, and it's your culture that shapes how they execute it.

Consider this:
- A company focused on innovation needs a culture that encourages risk-taking, creativity, and adaptability.

- A business driven by efficiency requires a culture that prioritizes structure, consistency, and accountability.

- A customer-centric organization thrives on a culture of empathy, responsiveness, and service excellence.

When culture and strategy align, something extraordinary happens: Your people don't just *follow orders*; they *live and breathe* your mission.

But here's the kicker: Company culture isn't just about who you are now. It's also about who you need to be to succeed in the future. This is where the concept of Strategic Company Culture takes center stage. It's about aligning your culture with your strategic objectives and ensuring that your people—at every level—are clear on how their behavior contributes to the big picture.

## Why Culture Fails (And How to Fix It)

The truth is most organizations fail to harness the power of culture. They get stuck in one of two traps:

### The Default Culture Trap:

This happens when culture develops organically without strategic intent. It becomes a patchwork of individual leadership styles, team dynamics, and historical habits—often riddled with contradictions. One team values collaboration, while another prizes competition. One leader encourages innovation, while another stifles it. The result? Confusion and friction.

**The "Fun at Work" Trap:**

Here, organizations focus on perks and benefits, believing they'll create a "great culture." But without deeper alignment to purpose and strategy, these surface-level efforts fail to sustain engagement or drive results. As the pandemic taught us, the "fun at work" culture crumbles when external challenges strip away the perks.

## *The Fix: Intentional, Strategic Culture*

To avoid these traps, organizations must intentionally design a culture that aligns with their strategic goals. This is where the concept of Strategic Company Culture comes into play—a culture that:

- Clarifies how people should work together to achieve business objectives.
- Aligns leadership, teams, and individual roles with the company's mission.
- Evolves as the organization's goals and priorities change.
- Helps define the right attitudes and aptitudes for talent acquisition.

## Culture as the Foundation of Employer Branding

Why start an employer branding book with a deep dive into culture? Because your culture is the DNA of your employer brand.

Think of it this way: Your employer brand is the story you tell, but your culture is the reality that backs it up. If there's a disconnect between the two, people will see through it instantly. In today's world of Glassdoor reviews and social media, you can't fake culture. To build a Magnetic Employer Brand, you must first recognize the elements of your culture that are truly worth branding. I like to think company culture is the "product" and the "service" we brand.

## The Link Between Culture and Talent Attraction

Here's where it gets exciting. When you articulate and live your culture, you create a natural filter for talent. The right people—those who thrive in your culture—are drawn to you like a magnet. At the same time, those who don't align with your values and ways of working self-select out. This isn't exclusionary; it's efficiency. It ensures that the people you hire are not only skilled but also a cultural fit.

## Culture as a Strategic Advantage

In a competitive talent market, culture is your ultimate differentiator. Competitors can copy your products, pricing, or perks, but they can't replicate your culture. This is why culture-driven organizations consistently outperform their peers. Research by Deloitte shows that organizations with strong cultures are:

- Three times more likely to attract top talent.
- Two and a half times more likely to retain employees.
- Two times more likely to achieve revenue growth.

And here's the kicker: Culture doesn't just benefit HR. It's a business-wide asset. A well-aligned culture improves customer satisfaction, drives innovation, and increases operational efficiency. When you build a Strategic Company Culture, you're not just building a great place to work— you're building a resilient, high-performing business.

## What You'll Learn in This Section

This chapter lays the groundwork for everything to come. In the next chapter, we'll explore Strategic Company Culture in depth, showing you how to align your culture with your business goals and make it the cornerstone of your Magnetic Employer Brand. From there, we'll dive into Employee Experiences, uncovering how to turn your people's stories into the most powerful marketing tool you've ever had.

This isn't just about attracting talent. It's about transforming your organization from the inside out. As you read on, you'll see why culture and experiences are the foundation of modern employer branding—and why The Magnetic Employer Branding Method™ is your key to unlocking their full potential.

## CHAPTER 2

# Strategic Company Culture

"*Strategy without culture is powerless. Culture without strategy is aimless.*"

UNKNOWN

I could have started this chapter with the famous strategy quote widely attributed to management consultant Peter Drucker: "Culture eats strategy for breakfast." While it's true that culture is a powerful force, in a modern business world, culture shouldn't eat strategy—it should amplify it. A company's culture must be carefully designed to serve its strategic goals, not exist as an independent, unbridled force. This is the essence of Strategic Company Culture.

If Chapter 1 framed culture as the personality of your organization, this chapter zooms in on the intentionality required to turn that personality into a competitive advantage. Strategic Company Culture connects the dots between who you are, why you exist, and how you work to achieve your goals. It's not about what's trendy or what makes your workplace seem fun—it's about building a culture that drives results, fosters clarity, and empowers your people.

Let's get real: Most companies don't have a Strategic Company Culture. What they have is a patchwork quilt of leadership styles, unwritten rules, and occasional bursts of enthusiasm. While this might keep the wheels turning, it doesn't drive a business forward. A Strategic Company Culture, on the other hand, is purpose-built to align with your business objectives and ensure that everyone—from the C-suite to the frontlines—is rowing in the same direction.

## Why Strategic Company Culture is a Game-Changer

The word "culture" often conjures up images of shared values, camaraderie, and rituals. While these elements matter, they are insufficient on their own. A culture that doesn't align with your strategy will feel directionless—a social club rather than a system of purpose.

Strategic Company Culture acts as a business's behavioral blueprint. It transforms lofty strategic ambitions into actionable, daily behaviors that everyone in the organization can understand and embrace. It:

1. **Aligns behavior with strategy:** By defining the behaviors required to meet business goals, it creates clarity and focus.
2. **Bridges the gap between leadership and employees:** It ensures that everyone understands their role in achieving the company's mission.
3. **Creates a common language:** It standardizes expectations, decision-making, and collaboration across teams.

In essence, Strategic Company Culture is the glue that binds your strategy to execution.

## The Cost of Misaligned Cultures

Let's consider what happens when culture and strategy don't align. Misalignment can manifest in various ways:

- **Confusion:** Employees don't understand how their work contributes to the organization's goals.
- **Frustration:** Contradictory behaviors between departments lead to inefficiency.

- **Turnover:** Talented employees leave because the culture fails to engage or inspire them.

Research by PwC found that 65 percent of employees cite organizational culture as more important than salary when evaluating job satisfaction. Meanwhile, Gallup data shows that disengaged employees cost the global economy $7.8 trillion annually in lost productivity. Misaligned culture isn't just an HR issue—it's a business crisis.

## Defining Strategic Company Culture

So, what makes a company culture "strategic"? The answer lies in its alignment with the organization's business strategy. Strategic Company Culture translates strategic goals into desired behaviors. These behaviors become the "how" of achieving the "what."

Let's break it down into its components:

1. **Purpose and Mission:** Why do you exist as a company? Your culture must embody and reinforce this purpose.
2. **Leadership Style:** What type of leadership behaviors are necessary to drive success?
3. **Workplace Behaviors:** How should employees approach their work to deliver on the strategy?
4. **Core Values:** What beliefs and principles guide decision-making?

A Strategic Company Culture is a performance-driven culture—it's not about pleasing everyone. It's about creating an environment where the right people thrive.

## The Four Strategic Culture Types (Based on the Competing Values Framework)

Developed by Robert E. Quinn and John Rohrbaugh, the Competing Values Framework reveals that successful cultures align with their strategic emphases. Here's a quick breakdown:

1. **Collaborative Culture (Clan):** Ideal for specialization strategies, where expertise, trust, mentoring, and teamwork are key.
2. **Innovative Culture (Ad-hocracy):** Perfect for organizations focused on creativity and agility, disruption and creativity.
3. **Control Culture (Hierarchy):** Drives efficiency optimization through structure and processes, therefore perfect for businesses and organizations prioritizing operational excellence and control.
4. **Competitive Culture (Market):** Designed for results-driven businesses aiming for market dominance.

None of these culture types aren't "good" or "bad." Instead, they're tools that enable you to achieve your strategy. The key is identifying which one best aligns with your business goals—and living it every day.

Let's dig deeper into Strategic Company Culture in action.

## Strategic Company Culture in Action

Here's where the power of this concept truly shines. Let's explore how companies operating in different strategic contexts can design distinct cultures to meet their needs.

## *1. The Collaborative Specialist Culture*

- **Business Strategy:** Specialization and expertise-driven services (e.g., consulting firms, law firms).
- **Cultural Characteristics:** Open communication, mentorship, knowledge sharing.
- **Leadership Model:** Flat hierarchy, with leaders acting as coaches rather than decision-makers.
- **Team Leader's Strategic Role:** Building and fostering teamwork and collaboration, empowering teams, providing mentoring and coaching, enabling success, sharing knowledge, and maintaining mutual trust.
- **HR's Strategic Role:** Building a culture of coaching and fostering knowledge and camaraderie as key strategic assets.
- **General Staff Profile:** Subject matter experts driven by a passion for lifelong learning and a commitment to being recognized as loyal team players.
- **Outcomes:** Employees feel empowered to contribute, leading to deeper client and interpersonal relationships and loyalty, and higher-quality outcomes.

## 2. The Innovative, Agile Culture

- **Business Strategy:** Disruption through innovation (e.g., tech startups, R&D-heavy companies).

- **Cultural Characteristics:** Entrepreneurial spirit, risk-taking, freedom to experiment.

- **Leadership Model:** Visionary and inspiring, with a tolerance for failure as part of the process.

- **Team Leader's Strategic Role:** Inspiring a shared vision, fostering innovation, encouraging experimentation, engaging customers, strengthening innovation skills, leading innovation efforts, empowering individuals, and driving continuous renewal.

- **HR's Strategic Role:** Serving as a change agent, driving transformation and managing expectations effectively.

- **General Staff Profile**: Entrepreneurial-minded innovators, developers, and change-makers who are passionate about customers and motivated by mission and purpose.

- **Outcomes:** A pipeline of creative ideas, faster product development, and market agility.

## 3. The Results-Driven Competitive Culture

- **Business Strategy:** Market dominance and growth (e.g., retail giants, sales-focused companies).

- **Cultural Characteristics:** Results oriented, competitive, customer focused.
- **Leadership Model:** Goal driven, emphasizing accountability and rewards.
- **Team Leader's Strategic Role:** Setting measurable and ambitious goals, driving achievement, monitoring the competitive landscape, ensuring excellent customer experiences, and celebrating victories.
- **HR's Strategic Role:** A business-focused, goal-oriented partner for leaders and a skilled expert in rewards and recognition.
- **General Staff Profile:** Ambitious and performance-driven professionals who thrive in competitive environments and maintain a strong focus on customer satisfaction.
- **Outcomes:** High performance, aggressive sales growth, strong brand and customer loyalty.

## 4. The Process-Oriented Control Culture

- **Business Strategy:** Operational efficiency and reliability (e.g., manufacturing, logistics).
- **Cultural Characteristics:** Structured, systematic, and rule oriented.
- **Leadership Model:** Centralized decision-making, focusing on process adherence.
- **Team Leader's Strategic Role:** Organizing and coordinating work, managing systems and processes, monitoring and reporting performance.

- **HR's Strategic Role:** Administrative human resources expert specializing in process control and cost management.
- **General Staff Profile**: A detail-oriented and meticulous quality assurer who thrives in the structure and security of hierarchical decision-making, rules, and regulations.
- **Outcomes:** Cost efficiency, consistent quality, and scalability.

These examples show that one size does not fit all. Your Strategic Company Culture should be as unique as your business model. What's more, most organizations are a combination of two or more strategic culture types with varying levels of emphasis, turning them into truly unique workplaces.

## How to Identify Your Strategic Company Culture

The process of identifying your Strategic Company Culture is not just an exercise in introspection—it's a pivotal business move that translates your organizational strategy into actionable behaviors. It's about discovering the heartbeat of how your company operates and aligns to achieve its goals.

Many organizations fall into the trap of adopting a generic "fun-at-work" culture or misaligning their cultural efforts with their strategic needs. That's where Strategic Company Culture sets itself apart—it's designed to serve as the foundation for sustainable business success. I have prepared an extra resource that will help you get started with identifying your Strategic Company Culture. More information on this in the Sources, References, and Resources section at the end of this book.

## *The Key Questions to Start With*

To begin identifying your Strategic Company Culture, here are some guiding questions to consider:

- **What is our business strategy?** Identify the core emphasis of your strategy: Is your business focused on innovation, operational excellence, market leadership, or customer intimacy?

- **What behaviors and attitudes** are critical to achieving our goals? Think about the skills, decision-making processes, and work ethics that your business relies on to thrive.

- **How do we define success?** Does success mean launching disruptive products quickly, ensuring flawless operational execution, or excelling in customer service?

- **What leadership style supports our strategy?** For example, innovative businesses might thrive under visionary leadership, while operationally efficient businesses may require leaders who excel in process management.

## The Role of Strategic Company Culture in Employer Branding

Here's the aha moment: Your employer brand is simply the outward expression of your culture. Without a well-defined culture, your employer brand will be vague, inconsistent, and unconvincing.

When you articulate your Strategic Company Culture, you:

- **Define your differentiators:** What makes your organization unique in the talent market?

- **Empower leadership to match your strategy:** Ensure your leadership model aligns with your business strategy and fosters a leadership style that empowers employees. The right leaders attract and retain the talent your business needs to achieve its defined success.

- **Attract the right talent:** People who thrive in your culture are naturally drawn to you.

- **Retain your best people:** Employees who align with your culture feel a sense of belonging and purpose.

A strong Strategic Company Culture also builds trust. It shows candidates and employees that your promises aren't just marketing fluff—they're backed by an authentic way of working.

## The Future of Work Demands Strategy-Driven Cultures

The workplace is evolving faster than ever. Hybrid models, automation, and global talent competition are reshaping how we work. In this environment, only organizations with clear cultural blueprints will thrive.

Your culture must not only reflect your strategy but also adapt to future challenges. This means embedding agility, resilience, and inclusivity into your Strategic Company Culture.

## A Note on Diversity, Equity, and Inclusion (DEI)

Strategic Company Culture is incomplete without DEI. Diverse teams drive better decision-making, creativity, and financial performance. Equity and inclusion ensure that your culture resonates with a broader spectrum of talent, making it a driver of both innovation and social impact.

## Why This Chapter Matters

This chapter isn't just a theoretical exploration of culture—it's a call to action. If you want your employer brand to attract the best talent, if you want your people to thrive, and if you want your business to dominate its market, you must invest in designing and nurturing a Strategic Company Culture.

This book introduces you to The Magnetic Employer Branding Method™, where your Strategic Company Culture becomes the backbone of your talent attraction and retention strategy. By storifying your culture, you transform it into a magnetic force that draws the right talent to your business.

- **For C-Suite Executives:** This approach bridges the gap between strategy and execution, ensuring every employee's role contributes to the big picture and every line manager is better equipped with bridging that gap through their leadership practices and communication.

- **For HR and Employer Branding Teams:** It provides clarity on who you should attract, reward, and promote, and why.

- **For Talent Acquisition Professionals:** It simplifies recruitment by highlighting the traits and values that matter most to your organization.

The organizations that master Strategic Company Culture are the ones that will win in the future of work. Don't just build a culture—build the culture your strategy demands.

The next chapter will explore how employee experiences— how your people feel about working within this culture—are the social proof that will amplify your Magnetic Employer Brand.

## CHAPTER 3

# Employee Experiences: The Proof in Your Employer Brand Pudding

*"Employee experience
drives customer
experience."*

TONY HSIEH

L et's be clear: An employer brand without great employee experiences is just a pretty façade. Employee experiences (EX) are the real-world proof that your culture works. They answer questions like:

- How do people feel about working here?
- Are they inspired by our mission and values?
- Do they feel supported, seen, and motivated to excel?

If your employees can't answer these questions positively, no amount of employer branding campaigns will succeed. In today's world of instant communication and viral opinions, your employee and candidate experiences are your ultimate credibility check.

## What Employee Experiences Really Mean

Employee experiences aren't about free snacks and cappuccino or hosting holiday parties. These perks are fine, but they don't define a meaningful workplace. Great employee experiences are about creating an environment where employees feel valued, motivated, and connected. They don't just boost morale—they drive performance, engagement, and advocacy. And in the world of employer branding, advocacy is everything.

At its core, employee experience covers the entire journey an employee takes with your organization, from the first day to their farewell—and even beyond.

Let's break it down into four key areas:

1.  **Performance Experiences:** The support, tools, and feedback employees need to succeed in their roles.

2.  **Engagement Experiences:** The motivation, emotional connection, and energy employees bring to their work.

3.  **Emotional Experiences:** How employees feel about their leaders, teams, and alignment with your values.

4.  **Pride Experiences:** The sense of belonging and fulfillment that inspires employees to promote your company.

## *The Ripple Effect of Employee Experiences*

When employees have positive experiences:

*   They become advocates, sharing glowing reviews and recommending your company to their network.

*   Their engagement drives higher productivity, innovation, and retention.

*   Their stories seamlessly align with your employer brand, making it authentic and trustworthy.

But when experiences are negative:

*   Employees disengage, leading to higher turnover and lower morale.

- Unfiltered reviews on platforms like Glassdoor and LinkedIn can tarnish your reputation.
- Your employer branding efforts fall apart as real-life experiences contradict the stories you're trying to tell.

## Candidate Experiences: The Often-Ignored Audience

Let's shift focus to an equally critical audience: your candidates. Think about this—if your company hires dozens or hundreds of people annually, the number of candidates engaging with your brand could be in the thousands. And these candidates:

- Are not yet loyal to your company and may never be.
- Have a powerful platform to share their experiences, good or bad.
- Expect clarity, speed, and respect during the recruitment process.

### *Why Candidate Experiences Matter*

Candidates' first interactions with your organization set the tone for your employer brand. A poor candidate experience—confusing applications, long silences, or robotic rejection emails—can have lasting consequences:

1. **Direct Damage:** Public grievances tarnish your reputation and make future hires more difficult.

2.  **Indirect Damage:** A ripple effect of negative sentiment deters potential applicants and spreads mistrust.

On the flip side, when candidates feel respected and valued—even if they don't get the job—they can become ambassadors for your brand. Clear communication, timely feedback, and personal touches create goodwill that amplifies your employer brand.

## The Overlooked Power of Employee and Candidate Experiences

Imagine spending months crafting a visually stunning employer branding campaign, complete with inspiring messaging and compelling storytelling. Then, imagine a Glassdoor review or LinkedIn post from a current or former employee that contradicts everything your employer brand claims to represent. Like it or not, your Employee and Candidate Experiences are half of your employer brand. They are the living, breathing testimonials that validate—or dismantle—your carefully crafted messaging.

In The Magnetic Employer Branding Method™, employee experiences are as critical as your Strategic Company Culture. While the Strategic Company Culture defines the "how we work here," Employee Experiences answer the question: "How do I feel about the way we work here?" These feelings directly shape perceptions, engagement, and, ultimately, the strength of your employer brand.

But here's the kicker: It's not just about your current and former employees. Your Candidate Experiences matter just as much, especially for companies that hire frequently or at scale. Candidates talk. Poor experiences—long hiring processes, lack of transparency, or robotic communication—can go viral online faster than any employer branding campaign can recover from. And because candidates are typically at the beginning of their relationship with your brand, their first impressions are foundational.

## The Interconnection Between Strategic Company Culture and Employee Experiences

Your Strategic Company Culture is the "blueprint" for how your organization operates. Employee and Candidate Experiences are the human reactions to these expectations. The alignment—or misalignment—between them determines your employer brand's authenticity.

For example:

- If your culture promotes collaboration, but employees experience cutthroat competition, your brand loses credibility.

- If you claim to value innovation, but employees face endless bureaucracy, your message falls flat.

- If your candidate process highlights "respect for people," but applicants feel ignored, your brand risks irrelevance.

This alignment between culture and experiences isn't optional; it's foundational to The Magnetic Employer Branding Method™. It's not just about telling a story; it's about delivering on the promises in that story.

## *The Magnetic Power of Aligning Culture and Experiences*

When you align your Strategic Company Culture with your Employee and Candidate Experiences, magic happens.

- It's authentic. Your employer brand becomes a true reflection of what it's like to work with you.

- It's strategic. Culture and experiences work together to achieve business goals, not just employee satisfaction.

- It's magnetic. The right people—those who thrive in your environment—are naturally drawn to you.

Remember, your employees and candidates are your most influential storytellers. Their experiences—positive or negative—define how the world perceives you as an employer. When employees feel proud, inspired, and fulfilled, they naturally share their stories, creating a ripple effect that attracts like-minded talent.

## How to Measure and Improve Employee and Candidate Experiences

To create an authentic, competitive, and Magnetic Employer Brand, you need to measure and improve experiences continuously. Here's how:

1. **Survey Employees Regularly:** Use tools like Culture Amp or Moticheck to gather insights on how employees feel.

2. **Monitor Review Sites:** Pay attention to platforms like Glassdoor and LinkedIn to spot patterns in feedback.

3. **Gather Candidate Feedback:** Include follow-up surveys post-interview to understand their experience.

4. **Use Data Analytics:** Measure key metrics like time-to-hire, offer acceptance rates, and employee retention.

5. **Establish an "Experience Task Force":** Create a cross-functional team to identify and resolve experience gaps.

## A Modern Take on Candidate and Employee Experiences

The Magnetic Employer Branding Method™ positions Employee and Candidate Experiences as essential building blocks for employer branding. They're not just nice-to-haves—they're critical to your success:

- **Employee Experiences:** The emotional backbone of your brand, providing stories and advocates that make your message credible.
- **Candidate Experiences:** The first impression that defines whether someone engages with or warns others about your brand.

## *The Risk of Ignoring This*

Failing to address Employee and Candidate Experiences isn't just risky—it's a missed opportunity:

- **Reputation Damage:** Negative reviews and online grievances can ripple across your industry.
- **Financial Losses:** Disengaged employees cost companies billions in lost productivity annually (Gallup).
- **Talent Drain:** Poor candidate experiences make it harder to attract top talent, putting your business at a disadvantage.

## Why This Chapter Matters

This chapter isn't just about insights; it's a call to action. By aligning your culture, Employee Experiences, and Candidate Experiences, you can create a brand that's magnetic—not just to employees, but to the entire world.

It's time to stop viewing Employee and Candidate Experiences as HR's responsibility or a recruitment checkbox. They are the core of your brand and the foundation of your business success.

> "Customer experience will never
> exceed employee experience."
> UNKNOWN

Great companies know this truth. Make Employee and Candidate Experiences exceptional, and your brand will shine brighter than ever.

# THE MASTER PLAN: YOUR MAGNETIC EMPLOYER BRAND STRATEGY

## CHAPTER 4

# The Transformative Employer Branding Mission Statement

*"A good mission statement should be able to fit on a T-shirt and be easily understood by a caveman."*

DONALD MILLER

I n today's competitive talent market, the companies that thrive are those with a clear sense of purpose and direction—not just as businesses but as employers. The Transformative Employer Branding Mission Statement is your North Star in employer branding, guiding your efforts and keeping your team focused on a shared vision of success.

Unlike your company's public mission or vision statements, this is an internal tool designed to clarify why you're investing in employer branding and what transformation you aim to achieve as an employer. Of course, you may use it as a replacement to employee value propositions, but make sure it is clear enough that it won't be mistaken as your company's mission statement.

## What is a Transformative Employer Branding Mission Statement?

Think of your employer brand vision as your organization's aspirational dream in the workplace context: the future you want to create for your employees, leaders, and talent pipeline. Now, think of your Transformative Employer Branding Mission Statement as the actionable framework for turning that dream into reality. It's a concise yet powerful articulation of:

1. What your employer brand seeks to accomplish (e.g., becoming the preferred employer for a specific audience or achieving an internal cultural transformation).

2. Who it serves (your employees, potential hires, and other stakeholders in your talent ecosystem).

3. How it aligns with your business's broader mission and goals.

While your employer brand vision outlines your long-term aspiration, the mission statement is your strategy's heartbeat, driving every decision and initiative.

## Why is it Transformative?

The mission statement isn't just about defining what you do as an employer; it's about identifying how your employer brand will evolve to meet the future needs of your business and talent audiences. Employer branding in the modern world isn't static—it's dynamic, responding to changes in workforce expectations, industry shifts, and cultural trends. A well-crafted Transformative Employer Branding Mission Statement ensures your efforts remain relevant, actionable, and adaptable.

**How to Craft Your Transformative Employer Branding Mission Statement**

1. **Start with Your Employer Brand Vision**
   - Begin by articulating what success looks like for your employer brand in three to five years.
   - Envision the Employee Experiences, leadership culture, and talent perceptions you want to cultivate.
2. **Gather Perspectives**

- Interview key stakeholders, your employees, but also talent acquisition (and HR, if you are not the HR), team leaders, and top management to gather insights on:
  - Employee satisfaction and engagement.
  - Candidate perceptions and recruitment challenges.
  - Business strategies and future growth plans.
- Use this input to ensure your mission statement aligns with both internal realities and external ambitions.

3. **Define Your Purpose**

- What is the core reason your organization is investing in employer branding?
- Is it to attract a specific type of talent, transform your leadership culture, merge acquired businesses and employees into your core organization, or establish a more inclusive workplace?

4. **Focus on the Outcome**

- What transformation will your employer branding efforts drive?
- How do you want to be known as an employer in the future?

5. **Keep it Concrete and Actionable**

- Avoid vague, generic language. A great mission statement is detailed and specific, providing clear direction for your employer branding strategy.

## *The Power of Clarity: Why Specificity Matters*

One of the biggest pitfalls in employer branding is creating statements that are too abstract or general to guide meaningful action. Imagine trying to build a skyscraper without blueprints—it's nearly impossible. Your Transformative Employer Branding Mission Statement acts as the blueprint for your efforts, ensuring alignment across your team and stakeholders.

By making the statement concrete and actionable, you give your employer branding team a clear focal point, allowing them to prioritize initiatives, craft aligned messaging, and evaluate progress effectively. This clarity also simplifies stakeholder buy-in, as leaders can easily see how the mission supports broader business goals.

## Crafting a Mission That Drives Action

A mission statement is only as valuable as its clarity and focus. Donald Miller, author of *Business Made Simple*, argues that many mission statements fail because they are too abstract. To make your Transformative Employer Branding Mission Statement truly transformative, it must articulate the "why." Why does this mission matter? Why is it worth the investment of time, effort, and resources? A compelling "why" resonates with stakeholders and keeps your team motivated.

For example:

- "Because our mission to innovate healthcare technology depends on attracting and retaining the brightest minds in [specific industries or segments] with [desired aptitudes and attitudes]."
- "Because creating an inclusive culture will help us better innovate, stay ahead of competition, and deliver our customer promise in our diverse customer base."

When your "why" aligns with your broader business purpose, it becomes easier to rally your team and secure leadership buy-in.

## Where Does the Transformative Employer Branding Mission Statement Fit?

While your employer brand vision provides inspiration, the Transformative Employer Branding Mission Statement is the foundation of your Master Plan. It sets the tone for all subsequent sections, including Key Story Themes, communication strategies, and metrics for success.

## *Examples of Transformative Employer Branding Mission Statements*

To spark your imagination, here are some examples of Transformative Employer Branding Mission Statements that balance clarity, ambition, and action, and focus on the "why":

- "[A company name] will create a workplace culture thriving on innovation, inclusivity, and integrity by 2026, empowering every employee to build a brighter future—because when people feel valued and inspired, they deliver their best work to transform industries and communities."

- "[A company name] will revolutionize the healthcare industry by 2027 through a purpose-driven, collaborative, and transparent workplace that attracts and retains top talent—because advancing healthcare outcomes depends on empowered people working together for the greater good."

- "[A company name] is on a mission to become the most trusted tech employer by 2025, fostering a culture of continuous learning, leadership excellence, and sustainable growth—because the world's most pressing problems require talented teams with the vision and skills to solve them."

- "[A company name] will redefine the future of digital marketing by 2026 by creating a workplace that inspires creativity, celebrates diversity, and nurtures talent—because authentic storytelling and innovation begin with empowered teams who reflect the world they serve."

- "[A company name] is transforming the manufacturing industry by 2028, leveraging cutting-edge technology, exceptional leadership, and a shared commitment to sustainability— because building a better, more sustainable world starts with empowering the people who make it possible."

Each example connects the employer brand to broader organizational goals while emphasizing the transformation the company seeks to achieve.

## From Mission to Momentum

Your Transformative Employer Branding Mission Statement is more than words on a page. It's a rallying cry for your employer branding team, a compass for your stakeholders, and a declaration of your organization's commitment to being a Magnetic Employer. By grounding your efforts in this mission, you set the stage for a brand story that captivates, connects, and converts—both internally and externally.

Now, it's time to roll up your sleeves and craft your own statement. Remember, this isn't just an exercise in branding— it's a transformative process that will define how your organization evolves in the eyes of its most valuable asset: its people.

# Employer Branding Goals, Objectives, and KPIs
### (Key Performance Indicators)

*"The base of the pyramid, the most important layer, is INTENTION. What change are you seeking to make? Does the team have clarity, measurements, and resources to prioritize this?"*

SETH GODIN

W hat does success look like in employer branding? Many struggle to answer this question because the metrics often overlap with recruitment or social media analytics. However, employer branding has its own unique objectives tied to long-term strategic goals. Unlike recruitment campaigns, which focus on short-term hiring needs and tactical campaign metrics and tend to reflect visibility rather than value, employer branding is about positioning your organization as the top choice for strategically vital talent—today and tomorrow.

**The Magnetic Employer Branding Method™ centers on three primary goals derived from the Talent Journey of the Information Era™ (TJIE):**

1. **Growing Employer Awareness:** Clarifying how your organization is perceived as an employer and ensuring you're recognized by relevant audiences.

2. **Building Employer Brand Affinity:** Creating deep emotional connections that make your organization the most preferred employer in your target market.

3. **Converting Employer Brand Value:** Turning your employer branding efforts into measurable returns on investment (ROI) for the business.

## Growing Employer Awareness

### What it Means

Growing employer awareness is about getting noticed by the right talent and ensuring your employer image is distinct, relevant, and aligned with your business goals. A strong employer awareness phase ensures that when talent in your strategic target audience thinks of potential employers, your organization is one of the first to come to mind.

## Building Employer Brand Affinity

### *What it Means*

Employer brand affinity goes beyond awareness—it's about creating a deep emotional bond between your organization and your talent audience. Affinity ensures your organization isn't just recognized but becomes the top choice in the minds and hearts of strategically vital talent. Affinity drives loyalty, trust, and advocacy, making your employer brand magnetic.

In essence, affinity means your audience doesn't just know you—they prefer you, over and over again. This preference shows up when candidates respond to your recruitment messages, employees choose to stay despite external offers, and your talent audience becomes vocal advocates of your brand, even if they've never worked for you.

Imagine being an employer that graduates dream about long before they enter the job market. They follow your updates, talk about your leadership culture with admiration, and list you as their "dream company" to work for—whether today or five years from now.

Or, what if you were the employer that seasoned professionals in your industry aspire to join, not because they're actively seeking a new job, but because they see your organization as the pinnacle of what a fulfilling, meaningful career could be? They discuss your innovative projects over coffee with peers, admire your leadership style in panel discussions, and follow your company updates, waiting for the perfect moment when their career path aligns with an opportunity at your organization. You're not just a workplace—they see you as the next natural step in their professional evolution.

These are definitions of employer *brand affinity*.

## *Why it Matters*

Strong employer brand affinity directly influences recruitment and retention costs, improves the quality of hires, and strengthens internal advocacy. Affinity is the linchpin that turns an employer brand into a competitive advantage, ensuring the organization is not competing for talent but attracting it organically.

Think of Apple in the tech space, or Patagonia in sustainability. Employees and prospects don't just see these companies as employers; they feel connected to their mission, values, and purpose. They want to be part of the story.

The affinity phase requires personalization and meaningful interaction. While awareness is about visibility, affinity is about connection. Use storytelling to show real, relatable employee experiences that align with the values of your target audience. Host exclusive events, provide value-add content like mentorship opportunities, or facilitate community-driven campaigns that position your organization as a caring, authentic employer.

# Converting Employer Brand Value (ROI)

## *What it Means*

Value conversions are the tangible outcomes of your employer branding efforts—your ROI (return on investment). They're the business benefits your organization gains as a result of building a strong employer brand. This is the payday that justifies the resources invested in employer branding.

Unlike tactical marketing conversions (e.g., social media clicks or newsletter subscriptions), ROI focuses on long-term, strategic outcomes such as reduced hiring costs, higher retention rates, or improved employee productivity.

ROI matters because C-suite executives and business leaders need to see the value of employer branding in terms of dollars saved, performance improved, and risks reduced. By clearly defining and delivering ROI, you ensure employer branding is seen as a strategic, indispensable business function—not just a marketing exercise.

To help you achieve these goals, this chapter explains how to set clear objectives and measurable KPIs, breaking down what each of these terms means and how to apply them in practice.

## Goals, Objectives, and KPIs: A Clear Distinction

### *Goals*

Think of goals as the long-term outcomes you aspire to achieve—the destination. They are high level and focus your efforts on where you need to go. The goals in employer branding are consistent across all organizations applying this methodology, as they all align with the stages of the Talent Journey of the Information Era™.

**Employer Branding Goals:**

- Growing employer awareness to ensure a distinct and recognizable employer image.

- Building employer brand affinity to foster emotional connections and loyalty with target talents and become the most preferred employer in the relevant target segments or industries.

- Converting specific employer brand value to deliver measurable ROI for the business.

### *Objectives*

Objectives are milestones—specific, actionable steps that move you closer to your goals. They provide focus, guide resource allocation, and enable measurable progress. While goals are universal, objectives should be tailored to your organization's strategic priorities.

**Example Objectives**

- Employer awareness:
  - o Increase followers on LinkedIn by 20 percent within six months to grow visibility among engineering students.
  - o Create and distribute twelve employer brand content pieces monthly to increase audience engagement.
- Employer brand affinity:
  - o Increase employee-generated posts and testimonials by 30 percent within the next year to foster greater employee pride and advocacy.
  - o Achieve a 25 percent boost in internal survey responses showing that employees feel aligned with and motivated by the company's strategic direction.
  - o Increase employee participation in cross-departmental collaboration initiatives by 20 percent, especially after a major company merger, to strengthen cultural integration.

I will take you through value conversions separately, as I want to emphasize their vital role for C-suite and the value of employer branding.

# KPIs (Key Performance Indicators)

KPIs are measurable metrics that indicate whether you're on track to meet your objectives. Unlike tactical metrics, which focus on short-term actions (e.g., social media clicks), KPIs reflect strategic progress.

## Examples of KPIs

- Employer awareness:
    o Number of relevant LinkedIn (or other social media) followers gained monthly.
    o Engagement rate on LinkedIn posts targeted toward engineering students (likes, shares, comments).
    o Percentage of engineering student profiles engaging with LinkedIn posts (can use LinkedIn audience demographics for this).
    o Number of content pieces published per month.
    o Engagement rate (clicks, likes, shares, comments) on employer brand content.
    o Website traffic generated from employer branding posts.
- Employer brand affinity:
    o Increase in employee referrals as a percentage of total hires.

o Year-over-year improvement in employer net promoter score (eNPS).

o Number of employee-generated posts/ testimonials shared monthly.

o Engagement rate (likes, shares, comments) on employee-generated posts.

o Sentiment analysis of employee-generated posts (positive vs. neutral vs. negative).

o Positioning in the annual national employer branding study in the relevant industry and among relevant competition.

o Internal survey participation rate.

o Percentage increase in "alignment with company strategy" scores in employee surveys.

## The Real Power of ROI in Employer Branding

The concept of return on investment (ROI) goes beyond recruitment metrics like time-to-fill or cost-per-hire. It addresses the larger pain points that hit the CEO's radar and impact the overall business. When employer branding is done well, it tackles these pain points and delivers measurable business value.

## *Why Employer Branding ROI Matters at the CEO Level*

The CEO and C-suite are not typically concerned with tactical marketing metrics like clicks or shares. Their focus is on outcomes that affect the company's performance and competitive edge, such as:

- **Missed Sales Targets:** If sales teams are understaffed, it directly impacts revenue. A strong employer brand ensures that critical roles are filled quickly, allowing teams to meet their goals.

- **Declining Customer Satisfaction:** High employee turnover or disengaged teams often lead to poor customer experiences. A strong employer brand helps attract and retain employees who deliver exceptional service.

- **Rising Turnover Costs:** Replacing high-performing employees is expensive and disruptive. Employer branding creates a magnetic culture that retains top talent, reducing churn and associated costs.

When you position employer branding as a solution to these critical business challenges, it becomes a strategic investment rather than a nice-to-have initiative.

## Examples of Employer Branding ROI: Objectives and KPIs

### 1. Reducing Cost of Hire

Strong employer brands attract pre-qualified talent, reducing reliance on expensive paid ads or headhunting services. This results in shorter time-to-hire and a significant decrease in recruitment costs.

**Objective:** Achieve a 30 percent reduction in external recruitment spend within eighteen months.

**KPI:** Year-over-year decrease in cost-per-hire and total annual recruitment spending.

### 2. Decreasing Employee Turnover

By aligning talent with your company's mission, values, and leadership culture, you retain employees longer, especially during probation periods, where mismatches often surface.

**Objective:** Reduce probationary turnover rates from 20 percent to 10 percent within one year.

**KPI:** Monthly retention rate of new hires in strategic roles.

### 3. Improving Customer Experiences

When employees resonate deeply with your mission and values, it shows in their work—especially in customer-facing roles. This improves the customer journey and strengthens the overall brand.

STORY-DRIVEN EMPLOYER BRANDING

**Objective:** Increase Net Promoter Score (NPS) by fifteen points within two years.

**KPI:** Quarterly NPS scores and customer satisfaction metrics.

## 4. Enhancing Stakeholder Trust

A strong employer brand reassures investors, customers, and partners during times of transformation (e.g., leadership changes, M&As).

**Objective:** Maintain investor confidence with consistent external messaging about leadership vision and cultural alignment.

**KPI:** Positive stakeholder sentiment in annual reputation audits.

## 5. Driving Strategic Talent Outcomes

A strong employer brand positions the organization to attract mission-critical talent who can drive innovation, growth, and transformation.

**Objective:** Ensure that 50 percent of new hires in key growth areas come from organic employer branding leads by the end of the next fiscal year.

**KPI:** Percentage of hires attributed to employer branding channels (e.g., employee referrals, inbound applications).

To make employer branding an indispensable part of your business strategy, you must define success in terms that matter to the business:

- **Value Created:** Reduced costs, higher productivity, improved brand reputation.
- **Impact Delivered:** Stronger customer experiences, better retention, and aligned talent.

When done well, ROI ensures that employer branding isn't just a cost—it's a competitive advantage that drives growth, innovation, and profitability.

## Tangible Examples of ROI

### Scenario: Stabilizing During a Merger

A company undergoing a merger faced high employee turnover because of cultural uncertainty. By implementing a Magnetic Employer Branding strategy:

- They retained 85 percent of employees during the merger (against an industry average of 60 percent).
- Internal advocacy increased by 40 percent, reducing the need for external hires.
- Customer satisfaction scores improved by ten points because of seamless employee integration.

### Scenario: Reducing Time-to-Hire

A high-growth tech company struggled with prolonged vacancies in key roles. By building employer brand affinity with engineering graduates and professionals:

- Time-to-hire decreased by 35 percent within one year.

- Recruitment costs dropped by $250,000 annually as reliance on headhunters decreased.

- The company attracted passive talent previously unreachable, leading to a 20 percent increase in high-performing hires.

## Strategic vs. Tactical Conversions: Understanding the Difference and Connecting the Dots

When measuring employer branding success, it's critical to differentiate between tactical conversions and strategic conversions. Both play distinct roles, but they serve different purposes in the overall strategy.

## *Marketing Conversions: KPIs to Indicate Impact and Progress*

Marketing conversions are the measurable actions and reactions your target audience takes in response to your employer branding efforts.

These include:

- Social media clicks, likes, comments, and shares.
- Newsletter sign-ups or career site visits.
- Downloading employer branding resources (e.g., e-books, videos, or podcasts).

- Following your employer brand accounts on social media platforms.
- Number of participants at your employer branding event.

These actions are essential because they indicate that your audience is engaging with your messaging and progressing along the Talent Journey of the Information Era™. Marketing conversions show that you're gaining momentum and building awareness or growing employer brand affinity, but they are not the ultimate measure of success. They help you understand whether your employer branding actions and activities are reaching and resonating with the right audience, but they are not directly valuable for the business. The objectives and KPIs for growing employer awareness and building employer brand affinity are marketing conversions, and the objectives and KPIs for value conversions (ROI) are strategic.

Think of marketing conversions as signposts on the road—they show you're heading in the right direction, but are not the destination itself.

## Strategic Conversions: The Destination

Strategic conversions are the endgame—the tangible outcomes that deliver real value to the organization and justify the employer branding investment. These conversions align with business goals and demonstrate how employer branding impacts the bottom line.

Examples include:

- **Reduced Time-to-Fill for Key Roles:** With a strong employer brand, pre-qualified candidates are more likely to be already in your talent pool, decreasing the time and cost needed to fill critical vacancies.

- **Increased Retention of High-Performing Employees:** Employer branding fosters a sense of belonging and alignment with the company's mission, reducing turnover and retaining top talent.

- **Improved Productivity and Morale:** Employees who are aligned with the company's values and culture tend to be more engaged, resulting in higher productivity and revenue per employee.

- **Enhanced Talent Quality:** Your employer brand attracts candidates who are not only skilled but are also the right fit for your culture, reducing the risk of mismatches and early turnover.

- **Strengthened Employer Advocacy:** Loyal employees become brand ambassadors, promoting the company to their networks, generating organic leads, and enhancing the company's reputation.

Strategic conversions demonstrate how employer branding moves the needle for the business—not just the marketing or recruitment team.

The real power of employer branding ROI lies in its ability to transform specific tactical wins into strategic business outcomes that resonate with leadership and align with the business's needs. It's not just about clicks—it's about the revenue saved or generated because you have the right people, in the right roles, at the right time.

By understanding this connection, you can plan goals and objectives that guide your employer branding work like signposts and expected ROI that communicate the value of employer branding to stakeholders in terms they care about, securing buy-in and resources to take your efforts to the next level.

## CHAPTER 6

# Defining Your Employer Brand's Target Audience

*"If you're marketing to everyone, you're reaching no one."*

UNKNOWN

When it comes to employer branding, one of the most misunderstood concepts is the target audience. Too often, companies confuse employer branding audiences with recruitment profiles, leading to vague, ineffective messaging that fails to attract the right talent. Here's the truth: Your employer brand target audience isn't everyone you might hire today. It's the group of people whose values, aspirations, and work personality align with your organization's mission, culture, and strategic business needs over the next few years to come.

Unlike recruitment profiles, which are crafted to address immediate hiring needs, employer brand target audiences are future focused. They represent the talents you want to attract over time—talents who will naturally gravitate toward your organization when the right opportunities arise because they already see your company as their preferred future employer. Building an employer brand isn't about harvesting applications today; it's about planting seeds for the future.

So, how do you identify and define this audience? How do you move beyond hiring profiles to build meaningful connections with the people who will power your business in the years ahead? Let's dive in.

## Who is in Your Talent Audience?

Your talent audience is broader than you might think. It includes:

- **Current employees**, whose experiences shape your brand story and help attract similar, like-minded talent.

- **Former employees**, whose opinions influence perceptions in the talent market—positively or negatively, depending on their experiences.

- **Job seekers**, whether they've applied to your roles, considered your vacancies, or interacted with your recruitment content.

- **Consultants and freelancers**, who work with your teams and assess your organization's culture and leadership during their collaborations.

- **Friends and family of employees**, who hear about your workplace culture through informal conversations and form secondhand impressions.

- **Customers and clients**, who often assess your organization as an employer based on their interactions with your people.

- **Recruitment agency audiences**, who temporarily enter your ecosystem during hiring campaigns and form impressions about your company through their experiences collaborating with your people and your applicants and candidates.

Why does this matter? Because all of these groups form opinions about your organization as an employer—even if they're not your primary target audience. Their word-of-mouth, online reviews, and casual comments all shape your reputation. Even if you're not actively working on employer branding, these perceptions are being formed every day. Understanding who these people are and how they see you is the foundation of building a Magnetic Employer Brand.

## *Why Defining Your Target Audience is Essential*

A message that tries to resonate with everyone ends up resonating with no one. Specificity is the secret to impactful employer branding. When you clearly define your target audience, you can craft messages that speak directly to their values, aspirations, and pain points. This specificity allows you to:

- **Build Meaningful Connections:** Tailored messages resonate emotionally, creating trust and affinity.

- **Improve Marketing ROI:** You reach the right people, in the right places, with the right content.

- **Drive Long-Term Results:** You position your brand as the natural choice for the talent you'll need in the future, not just today.

Building an employer brand is about more than raising awareness. It's about creating a lasting emotional connection with the talent that matters most to your organization. And that starts with defining exactly who they are.

Key Insight: Your employer brand is the sum of how your target audience feels about you. The more you understand them, the more you can influence those feelings—and the actions they take as a result.

# Employer Branding Audiences vs. Recruitment Profiles

The difference between employer branding audiences and recruitment profiles lies in their purpose and scope:

- Recruitment profiles are role specific. They help you identify and market to the ideal candidates for a current vacancy based on skills, experience, and immediate organizational needs—and often also what type of balance in skills, characteristics, and temperaments your existing team might need for best collaboration, enjoyment of work, and success.

- Employer branding audiences are broader and future focused. They represent the groups of talent whose values, behaviors, and aspirations align with your company's mission, culture, and strategic goals over the next few years. These people have the assets your business can benefit from, but they also need to relate with your "organization person" so that they feel compelled to use their attitude and aptitude in your company.

**Let's break it down with an example:**

- A recruitment profile might target a senior software engineer with five years of experience, expertise in Python, and a background in fintech.
- An employer branding audience would focus on broader segments like "innovative software

developers" or "collaborative tech talents," emphasizing shared values, mindsets, and aspirations that align with your company's culture and vision.

Recruitment marketing is about harvesting; employer branding is about planting and nurturing. When you focus only on the immediate hiring need, you limit your ability to attract the right people over the long term, and that is one specific advantage; employer branding can create what recruitment marketing cannot.

## Segmenting Your Employer Branding Audience

To define your employer branding audience, think beyond individual roles. Instead, focus on segments—groups of people who share common characteristics, values, and aspirations that align with your organization's mission and culture.

## *Step 1: Start with Strategic Business Needs*

Your employer brand must support your business's strategic goals. Look ahead two to three years. Is your organization planning to:

- Expand into new markets?
- Launch innovative products or services?
- Scale through mergers and acquisitions?

If you don't know, discuss with your C-suite, as this is vital.

These strategic priorities will dictate the types of talent you'll need to attract and retain. For example, a company entering a new market may prioritize talent with multilingual skills or regional expertise, while a business focused on product innovation may target engineers and creative problem-solvers.

Pro Tip: Reverse engineer from your business strategy. Ask: What types of talent will drive our success in the next few years?

## Step 2: Identify Key Talent Segments

List the broader talent groups your organization relies on. For example:

- Product development
- Sales
- Customer service
- Logistics
- Administration

Then, look for common denominators within these groups. For instance:

- Are they driven by innovation or collaboration?
- Do they value autonomy or teamwork?
- What shared aspirations align with your culture?

Think beyond roles and titles. Focus on behaviors, attitudes, and values that define your ideal talent.

## *Step 3: Use Psychographic Segmentation*

While demographic segmentation (age, location, education) is common in recruitment, psychographic segmentation goes deeper. It focuses on the psychological traits that drive behavior, such as values, aspirations, and work styles. Apply what matches with your company's mission, purpose, values, culture, business needs, customer promises, and leadership style. For example:

- **Innovators:** Curious, creative talents who thrive in fast-paced, innovative environments.
- **Collaborators:** Empathetic, team-oriented professionals who value connection and cooperation.
- **Achievers:** Goal-driven individuals who prioritize growth and results.

Psychographic segmentation allows you to align your employer brand with the deeper motivations and aspirations of your target audience, creating messages that resonate on a human level.

Key Insight: Psychographic segmentation transforms your employer brand from a one-size-fits-all approach to a personalized magnet for the right people. My podcast, Episode 109, taps into psychographic segmentation in employer branding. Go to Sources, References and Resources for more information on how to find my podcast.

## *Talent Personas: Bringing Your Audience to Life*

Once you've segmented your audience, the next step is to create Talent Personas—fictional, archetypical representations of your ideal talent segments. These personas help you humanize your audience, guiding your content creation and employer brand marketing.

## *How to Create Talent Personas*

1. **Demographics:** Age, life stage, professional background, current status of life, including needs, interests, and aspirations.
2. **Work Style:** Preferred ways of working, natural strengths, values, work personality, characters matching with your company culture and future needs.
3. **Pain Points:** Challenges they face in their careers or work-life balance hindering or stopping them from enjoying a fulfilling career and life.
4. **Aspirations:** What they want to achieve in their careers and lives.
5. **Media Habits, Interests, and Examples of How They Spend Their Time Outside Work:** Where they consume content (e.g., social media platforms, podcasts, blogs), what type of content they consume, and what else is consuming their minds and winning their sustainable attention.

For example, a Talent Persona might look like this:

### "Timothy The Talent Marketer"

**Personal background:**

- Age: twenty-eight to thirty-five.
- In a serious relationship.
- A homeowner or saving up for their own home in the city.
- Enjoys the hustle and bustle of city life with cinemas, theaters, museums, and restaurants.

**Current professional status and professional goals:**

- Education: Business graduate, majoring in human resource management or marketing.
- Current role: A talent acquisition manager in a fast-growing software product business that operates internationally, is headquartered in Finland, employs at least 250 people, and hires fifty-plus a year for technical roles.
- Responsible for daily sourcing and "selling" of the opportunity to join their company.
- Has worked in this role for about three years. Work is very repetitive and stressful because of the war for tech talent.
- Key skills: Using social media and the Internet for sourcing, evaluating talent profiles, selling the benefits of working for this company, closing

talent leads to the talent funnel, bilingual: English and Swedish.

- Reports to: HR manager.
- Career goals: Desires to work more with marketing and communication. Is interested in working in employer branding because of personal experiences with how lack of employer brand awareness affects the success of talent acquisition.
- Wants to develop his career in the direction of versatile talent marketing and continue to help fast-growth businesses succeed in talent acquisition and retention.
- Their Work-to-Life Riddle to be solved is that his current employer seems not to see value in employer branding and, therefore, has no opportunities to professionally develop in employer branding in his current workplace.
- Is development driven and looks for a concrete career development plan in the next workplace.

**Key Characteristics, Values, Working Style**

**Timothy values:**

- An opportunity to develop professional skills through courses and other learning opportunities provided by the employer.
- A salary that expresses the value of his role for the business, even though salary is not his primary motivator for selecting his next role. However, as

someone saving for his own home, he appreciates a reward system based on results/value generated for the business.

- An employer who invests in leadership and a healthy work atmosphere, good work-to-life balance and remote work opportunities.

**Timothy's character strengths:**

- Highly self-driven when in a position with clear goals and expectations and the ability to make decisions. Persistent in reaching goals.
- Good social skills and enjoys social connections and networking. A team worker.
- Excellent communicator, both written and spoken. Strives to make sure the message is taken well and understood.
- Great with the big picture.
- Ideas rich but also a doer and deliverer.

**Likely character weaknesses:**

- Only stays motivated if the role has been well defined and there are no progressive milestones on the horizon.
- Struggles if the ownership of the role is not clear and respected by other stakeholders.
- Finds it challenging if there are no social connections in the role and everyone works remotely all the time.

**Topics of interest, hobbies, preferred media, and usage of media:**

- Preferred communication: WhatsApp, email, Intranet, face-to-face; doesn't enjoy organizations where multiple communication apps interfere with the ability to concentrate.

- Uses the Internet and social media a lot for personal development, keeping current with news, updates, and industry-related and professional topics; knows and follows many industry influencers, podcasts, and YouTube channels and is up to date on relevant trends.

- Preferred social networking site: LinkedIn. Highly active user because of current role in talent acquisition.

- Enjoys cross-country skiing and parachuting as spare-time hobbies.

- Loves to solve puzzles and other brainteasers.

Talent Personas make your target audience tangible, enabling you to craft messages that feel personal and relevant. At the end of this book, in the Resources, I have a link to locate the downloadable Talent Persona template.

## Work-to-Life Riddles: The Hidden Motivators Behind Career Decisions

Have you ever wondered why talented individuals leave great jobs, or why some people stay in roles that seem uninspiring? The answer lies in what I call Work-to-Life Riddles—those subtle, deeply personal challenges or aspirations that influence how we think about our careers and lives. These riddles are not always obvious, even to the individuals experiencing them. They often build up over time, nudging someone toward change until one day they feel ready to act.

Understanding these riddles is the key to unlocking the motivations of your employer branding audience. They represent the intersection of personal and professional life, where work decisions are shaped not just by job responsibilities but by broader life goals, values, and circumstances. Unlike surface-level drivers like salary or location, Work-to-Life Riddles delve deeper into the emotional and psychological layers of career decisions. By addressing these riddles in your employer branding messages, you position your organization as a trusted guide for talent navigating their own journeys.

## *The Three Layers of Work-to-Life Riddles*

To fully grasp the power of Work-to-Life Riddles, it's helpful to think of them as multi-layered challenges. Each layer reflects a different kind of driver:

### 1. External Riddles

External riddles are the most visible and tangible. They are often circumstantial and situational, such as:

- Losing a job because of layoffs.
- Relocating because of a partner's new opportunity.
- Needing a job after graduation or parental leave.

These reasons might prompt someone to start looking for a new role, but they rarely dictate which role they'll choose. External riddles are the initial push, but they lack the emotional depth to create lasting engagement with your employer brand.

## 2. Inner Riddles

Inner riddles go deeper, addressing an individual's self-perception, values, and aspirations. These are the internal questions that shape how someone evaluates potential employers, such as:

- "Am I growing in my career, or am I stagnating?"
- "Does my work align with my values and identity?"
- "Am I proud to tell others where I work and what I do?"
- "Does my nearest manager provide me the support and encouragement I desire?"

These inner drivers are critical because they often determine why someone chooses one employer over another. When your employer brand resonates with these inner riddles—by offering growth, alignment, and pride—you become a magnet for the right talent.

## 3. Philosophical Riddles

At the deepest level, we find philosophical riddles—questions about ethics, purpose, and the bigger picture. These riddles are often tied to a person's sense of morality or long-term fulfillment, such as:

- "Am I contributing to something meaningful?"
- "Does this company align with my values and morals?"
- "Can I make a positive impact here?"
- "Is it fair how I'm being treated here?"
- "I deserve more than they are willing to offer."

Philosophical riddles are often the deciding factor for talents evaluating whether to stay with or leave an employer. They shape how individuals view their work as part of their life's legacy. Employers who can demonstrate alignment with these deeper motivations tend to attract and retain talent who are not just employees but passionate advocates.

## *How Work-to-Life Riddles Influence Career Transitions*

People don't wake up one day and decide to change jobs on a whim. The process of transitioning from a passive to an active job seeker is gradual, shaped by a combination of Work-to-Life Riddles building up over time.

Here's how the journey typically unfolds:

1. **The Buildup:** An individual starts to notice subtle signs of dissatisfaction—boredom, frustration, or a sense of misalignment with their work or company culture. These feelings often simmer below the surface for months or even years.

2. **The Trigger:** A specific event—a missed promotion, a change in leadership, or even a

conversation with a friend—brings these feelings to the forefront. The individual begins to actively consider change.

3. **The Exploration Phase:** The person starts exploring their options, not necessarily by applying for jobs but by researching potential employers, browsing LinkedIn, and paying closer attention to companies they admire.

4. **The Decision:** Once they find an employer whose values, culture, and opportunities align with their Work-to-Life Riddles, they take action—whether that means applying, networking, or simply following the company more closely.

Key Insight: Employer branding works best when it addresses the buildup and exploration phases, positioning your organization as the solution to Work-to-Life Riddles before the talent is ready to make a move.

## Common Work-to-Life Riddles and How to Address Them

Let's take a closer look at some of the most common Work-to-Life Riddles and how you can address them through your employer branding strategy:

### 1. Boredom

When work becomes monotonous, even the most loyal employees start to disengage. They crave new challenges, opportunities to learn, and projects that reignite their passion.

*Your Employer Brand Solution: Highlight growth opportunities, exciting projects, and your commitment to continuous learning. Showcase stories of employees who've transitioned into new roles or taken on innovative projects within your company.*

## 2. Leadership Disconnect

A poor relationship with a manager is one of the top reasons people leave jobs. Talents often stay for great leaders and leave when they feel unsupported or undervalued.

*Your Employer Brand Solution: Emphasize your leadership culture and the support systems you provide. Share content that highlights the mentorship and guidance employees receive from their managers, and be transparent about how you invest in leadership development.*

## 3. Cultural Misalignment

When employees feel they no longer "fit" within an evolving company culture, they start looking for organizations that align better with their values and work style.

*Your Employer Brand Solution: Be honest about your culture. Use your employer branding messages to showcase your values, ways of working, and the kind of environment you offer. Transparency helps attract people who will thrive in your culture while filtering out those who won't.*

## 4. Life Stage Changes

From becoming a parent to relocating for a partner's job, life stage changes often drive career decisions.

*Your Employer Brand Solution: Show how your company supports employees during major life transitions. Highlight flexible working arrangements, relocation support, and family-friendly policies in your content.*

### 5. Desire for Impact

Many talents, especially Millennials and Gen Zers, want to work for organizations that contribute to a greater good.

*Your Employer Brand Solution: Showcase your company's mission, social impact initiatives, and stories of how employees make a difference through their work. Create content that demonstrates your commitment to meaningful, purpose-driven business practices.*

## Using Work-to-Life Riddles to Shape Your Employer Branding

Understanding Work-to-Life Riddles isn't just about empathy; it's about strategy. These riddles give you a road map for creating employer branding content that speaks directly to the hearts and minds of your target audience.

Here's how to put this concept into action:

1. **Map the Riddles:** Identify the most common Work-to-Life Riddles faced by your target audience. Use surveys, interviews, and feedback from current employees to gather insights.
2. **Tell Stories That Resonate:** Craft narratives that show how your organization solves these riddles.

Highlight real-life employee stories that address boredom, leadership, culture, or other common challenges.

3. **Create a Continuous Dialogue:** Employer branding isn't a one-time campaign. Use social media, blogs, videos, and other channels to continuously share content that addresses your audience's Work-to-Life Riddles.

The Bottom Line: Work-to-Life Riddles are the bridge between where your target audience is and where they want to be. By understanding and addressing these riddles, you position your organization as the trusted guide who can help talent navigate their journeys. This isn't just employer branding—it's human branding. And it's what makes your brand magnetic.

## Applying the Insights

Defining your target audience is just the beginning. Once you've segmented your audience, created Talent Personas, and identified Work-to-Life Riddles, you can use these insights to:

- Craft more personalized and, therefore, resonant content.
- Choose the right channels to reach your audience.
- Build a narrative that positions your organization as the trusted guide in their journey.

Your target audience isn't just a demographic; it's a group of real people with real aspirations, challenges, and dreams. When you understand and speak to these, you don't just build a brand—you build relationships.

## CHAPTER 7

# The Modern Work-to-Life Promise: Redefining the Employee-Employer Connection

"The key to work-life balance is to not compartmentalize our lives, but to integrate them."

ARIANNA HUFFINGTON

I n an era where work and life are no longer confined to separate spheres, the concept of an employer value proposition (EVP) feels antiquated. While the original intent of EVPs was admirable—providing clarity on what employees could expect—they often lack the depth and specificity needed to resonate in today's work environment. Instead of serving as compelling differentiators, most EVPs devolve into vague generalizations, offering little insight into what truly sets an organization apart as an employer.

That's why I introduced the Modern Work-to-Life Promise as part of The Magnetic Employer Branding Method™. This evolved approach captures the reality of today's interconnected work-life landscape and focuses on the transformative value an employer brings to its employees— not just during working hours, but in their broader lives, today and into the future.

## The Evolution from EVP to Work-to-Life Promise

The traditional EVP often feels like a relic of the pre-digital age. In the early 2000s, with limited communication channels such as print ads and recruitment fairs, concise statements were necessary to convey employer promises. But the world has changed. Social media and digital platforms have created endless opportunities for storytelling, transparency, and ongoing communication. A static EVP no longer suffices.

The Modern Work-to-Life Promise shifts the focus from slogans to meaningful, ongoing communication. It's not a tagline or a one-time statement; it's a promise rooted in your organization's purpose, values, and leadership culture. This promise addresses the critical question every potential and current employee asks: How does working here make my life better today, and how does it help me create a brighter future for myself?

## *The Role and Importance of the Work-to-Life Promise*

### 1. It Reflects the Changing Nature of Work

Work-life boundaries have blurred because of digitalization, the pandemic, and global crises. Employees expect more than a paycheck; they seek meaning, support, and alignment between their professional and personal lives. The Work-to-Life Promise acknowledges this shift, offering a holistic view of how an employer contributes to its employees' overall well-being.

### 2. It Prioritizes Transparency and Authenticity

In a world where employees demand transparency, a shallow EVP can feel disingenuous. The Work-to-Life Promise, on the other hand, is deeply rooted in the lived experiences of your employees. It leverages real data—employee feedback, satisfaction surveys, and organizational strengths—to articulate a promise that feels authentic and achievable.

### 3. It Builds Trust Through Consistent Communication

Unlike a static EVP, the Work-to-Life Promise is a living commitment communicated through stories, content, and actions. It's not about crafting a perfect slogan; it's about creating an ongoing dialogue with your employees and talent audience, showing them how you consistently deliver on your promise.

### 4. It Aligns Internal and External Perceptions

The Modern Work-to-Life Promise bridges the gap between internal employee experience and external employer branding. It provides a framework for aligning your internal culture with the story you share with the outside world, ensuring consistency and authenticity in your employer brand.

## How to Craft Your Modern Work-to-Life Promise

Creating a Modern Work-to-Life Promise requires introspection, collaboration, and data-driven insights. Here's how to approach it:

### *Step 1: Start with Employee Insights*

Your promise must reflect reality. Use employee satisfaction surveys, feedback, and workshops to identify:

- What your employees value most about working at your organization.
- Strengths in your leadership culture, values, benefits, and opportunities.
- Weaknesses or gaps that need addressing to fulfill your promise.

- Opportunities for enhancing employee experiences.

## Step 2: Identify the Broader Impact

Move beyond workplace specifics to consider how your organization impacts employees' lives. Ask questions like:

- How does our leadership style support personal growth?
- What opportunities, support, and benefits do we offer for skill development, career advancement, and life enhancement?
- How do our mission and values align with employees' personal goals and aspirations?
- How do we support you living and building the kind of life you desire?

## Step 3: Build a Comprehensive Framework

Turn your findings into a SWOT analysis for your employer brand. This exercise highlights:

- Strengths to amplify.
- Weaknesses to address.
- Opportunities to innovate.
- Threats to mitigate.

This process ensures your promise is both aspirational and achievable.

## Step 4: Use the Promise as a Guiding Principle

Your Work-to-Life Promise should serve as a foundation for all employer branding activities. It's not just a section in your Master Plan; it's a lens through which all strategies, content, and decisions are evaluated.

# Examples of Modern Work-to-Life Promises

In Chapter 4, we discussed the Transformative Employer Branding Mission Statement, and I gave you some examples of what those could look like. I'm bringing them back into this chapter, in order not to confuse you with what may appear like another mission statement and instead help you align your Transformative Employer Branding Mission Statement for your employer branding team and your Modern Work-to-Life Promise for your internal and external target audience.

## Tech Employer

### Transformative Employer Branding Mission Statement:

"[A company name] is on a mission to become the most trusted tech employer by 2025, fostering a culture of continuous learning, leadership excellence, and sustainable growth—because the world's most pressing problems require talented teams with the vision and skills to solve them."

**Modern Work-to-Life Promise:**

"At [a company name], we believe that empowering people with knowledge and tools extends far beyond the office. Our culture of continuous learning and mentorship fosters not only professional growth but also personal independence and self-confidence. Whether you're developing new skills or leading groundbreaking projects, we promise to equip you with the financial and intellectual freedom to shape the life you want—today and in the future."

## Healthcare Innovator

**Transformative Employer Branding Mission Statement:**

"[A company name] will revolutionize the healthcare industry by 2027 through a purpose-driven, collaborative, and transparent workplace that attracts and retains top talent—because advancing healthcare outcomes depends on empowered people working together for the greater good."

**Modern Work-to-Life Promise:**

"When you join [a company name], you become part of a purpose-driven organization that values compassion, integrity, and teamwork. But we're just as committed to your life outside of work. From leadership programs designed to strengthen your decision-making to initiatives that promote mental and physical well-being, we promise to help you build a life of balance, resilience, and meaningful contribution to the world around you."

## *Digital Marketing Leader*

**Transformative Employer Branding Mission Statement:**

"[A company name] will redefine the future of digital marketing by 2026 by creating a workplace that inspires creativity, celebrates diversity, and nurtures talent—because authentic storytelling and innovation begin with empowered teams who reflect the world they serve."

**Modern Work-to-Life Promise:**

"[A company name] promises to celebrate your individuality and nurture your creative energy, both inside and outside the workplace. Through a culture of inclusivity and innovation, we provide opportunities that go beyond career advancement. Whether it's financial wellness programs, leadership training, or flexibility to support your passions, we're here to inspire your confidence and help you achieve independence in every area of your life."

## *Sustainable Manufacturer*

**Transformative Employer Branding Mission Statement:**

"[A company name] is transforming the manufacturing industry by 2028, leveraging cutting-edge technology, exceptional leadership, and a shared commitment to sustainability—because building a better, more sustainable world starts with empowering the people who make it possible."

**Modern Work-to-Life Promise:**

"At [a company name], sustainability is more than a business goal—it's a way of life we want to share with you. By fostering a culture of responsibility, collaboration, and growth, we promise to support you in building a life aligned with your values. From leadership that listens to benefits that prioritize your well-being and your family's future, our commitment is to help you thrive as you contribute to creating a better world."

## *The Unique Angle*

Each Work-to-Life Promise addresses:

1. **Values:** How the organization's core beliefs influence and improve employees' lives holistically.
2. **Culture:** The way of working, collaborating, and growing that shapes employees' personal and professional lives.
3. **Leadership Principles:** Specific leadership qualities or practices that foster confidence, independence, or resilience.
4. **Benefits and Initiatives:** Offerings tailored to enhance life beyond work, such as financial wellness, personal development, remote working options or family-oriented support.

This approach ensures that the Modern Work-to-Life Promise is truly transformative and distinct, positioning your company employer as a life-enhancing partner, not just a provider of jobs. It's a meaningful departure from conventional EVPs and aligns beautifully with my vision of employer branding as a holistic, human-centric strategy.

## From Promise to Practice

The Modern Work-to-Life Promise is not a one-time declaration—it's an ongoing commitment. Here's how to bring it to life:

- **Regular Content:** Share stories, videos, and examples of how your organization fulfills its promise.

- **Internal Alignment:** Use the promise to guide leadership practices, performance reviews, and employee engagement initiatives.

- **External Transparency:** Showcase how your promise differentiates your organization in the talent market, appealing to passive job seekers and future employees.

## Why the Work-to-Life Promise Matters

The Modern Work-to-Life Promise isn't just a rebranding of the EVP; it's a fundamental shift in how we think about the relationship between employers and employees. It reflects the realities of today's work environment, addresses the aspirations of modern talent, and provides a framework for building trust, loyalty, and engagement. By embracing this promise, your organization not only attracts top talent but also creates a meaningful and lasting impact on their lives— and that is the essence of a Magnetic Employer Brand.

## CHAPTER 8

# The Desired Employer Brand Perceptions: Shaping the Emotional DNA of Your Employer Brand

*"A brand is the set of expectations, memories, stories, and relationships that, taken together, account for a consumer's [or talent's] decision to choose one product or a service [or employer] over another."*

SETH GODIN

W hat makes your organization unforgettable in the eyes of top talent? How do you ensure your brand resonates deeply enough to win hearts and minds while inspiring trust and admiration? This is where desired employer brand perceptions come into play—a cornerstone of The Magnetic Employer Branding Method™.

Desired employer brand perceptions are the specific beliefs, feelings, and associations you want your target audience to connect with your organization. These perceptions don't arise by chance; they are intentionally designed, nurtured, and communicated through your employer branding efforts.

But here's the twist: These perceptions must be authentic, rooted in your culture, leadership style, and employee experiences. Otherwise, they're just empty promises— setting you up for mistrust and disappointment instead of admiration and affinity.

## Why Desired Employer Brand Perceptions Matter

Employer branding isn't just about being known; it's about being known for the right reasons. Desired perceptions allow you to:

1. Define your uniqueness in a crowded talent market.
2. Shape emotional connections that drive loyalty and advocacy.

3.  Tell a story that invites current and potential
    employees to join a journey aligned with their
    values, aspirations, and professional dreams.
4.  Communicate change in a way that excites rather
    than alienates.

When your desired perceptions align with the genuine
experiences you can deliver, you create a brand that
attracts, retains, and inspires talent who will thrive in your
organization. Perceptions, when authentic and distinctive,
lead to trust—and trust is the currency of modern employer
branding.

## How to Select Desired Employer Brand Perceptions

To be effective, your desired employer brand perceptions
must meet these criteria:

### 1. Rooted in Reality

Your perceptions must reflect who you truly are as an
organization—not an idealized version. If your culture
values transparency and autonomy, but leadership operates
in a command-and-control manner, you'll fail to align
perceptions with reality.

### 2. Reflective of Change or Growth

If your organization is undergoing transformation—
whether it's cultural, strategic, or operational—your desired
perceptions should align with the future state you're

building. Perceptions can help existing and future employees see themselves as part of this evolution.

For example:

- "We are leading the shift toward a more sustainable tech industry."
- "Here, people grow faster and achieve more because our leadership is committed to mentoring and development."

**3. Limited to a Few High-Impact Perceptions**

Focus is power. Aim for three to four key perceptions—no more. Why? Because your content and communication efforts must consistently and equally reinforce all chosen perceptions. Spreading yourself too thin dilutes your messaging and weakens your brand impact.

**4. Audience-Centric**

What does your audience truly care about? Too often, organizations lean into hype topics or vague corporate platitudes. Instead, focus on the needs and aspirations of your target talent. What motivates them? What are their biggest career and life challenges? How can you uniquely address them?

## Crafting Specific and Impactful Perceptions

Generic phrases like, "We are an innovative company," or "We value diversity," don't cut it. They're overused, impersonal, and fail to stand out.

When it comes to crafting desired employer brand perceptions, the focus must shift from what your company *thinks* it represents to what your talent audience *experiences* and *feels* about you. This subtle but vital distinction is the backbone of modern employer branding. Your desired perceptions should reflect how your external talent audience views your organization, not how you describe yourself.

In The Magnetic Employer Branding Method™, the talent is always the hero, and the employer is their guide. Think about how your ideal talent audience interacts with your brand: through your social media posts, recruitment campaigns, employee stories, or their personal experiences with your people at events or interviews. What impressions do these interactions leave on them? What do they tell their friends, peers, or mentors after encountering your brand?

Your desired employer brand perceptions should align with the authentic stories you share and the experiences you create for talent, making your organization stand out in their minds. Instead of focusing on what we are, think about what the talent sees, feels, and believes about working with your company.

This shift in perspective changes everything:
- From "We value transparency and innovation"
  - To "Their leadership style seems transparent and forward-thinking; they share insights that feel genuine and valuable."
- From "We provide growth opportunities for our employees"

o To "Based on their content, it looks like people at this company have real opportunities to grow and take on exciting challenges."

## Why Talent-Centric Perceptions Matter

By centering your messaging on the talent's perspective, you create an emotional connection. This approach acknowledges the talent's needs, aspirations, and values while positioning your company as a trusted partner in their career journey. It's not about shouting, "Look at us!" but quietly leaving impressions like:

- "This feels like the kind of workplace where I could thrive."
- "I get the sense they value people like me and what I bring to the table."
- "It seems like they care about making a positive impact, not just on their business but in the lives of their employees."

This methodology builds credibility and invites talent to visualize themselves as part of your story. Your goal is to create perceptions that speak directly to their dreams, challenges, and priorities.

## Examples of Desired Employer Brand Perceptions

To help you see how this works in practice, here are some desired employer brand perceptions crafted to resonate with talent, complemented with the examples from

Transformative Employer Branding Mission Statements and Modern Work-to-Life Promises:

## *For a tech company focused on diversity and innovation:*

**Talent Perception:**

*"From what I've seen, this company is leading the way in tech innovation and creating a space where diverse voices are genuinely valued and celebrated."*

**Matching Modern Work-to-Life Promise:**

*"Empowering diverse innovators to thrive, contribute, and create a better future through technology."*

## *For a health-tech company revolutionizing patient care:*

**Talent Perception:**

*"The way they share their employee stories, it's clear they're deeply invested in making a real impact on healthcare and patient well-being. It feels like a place where purpose drives everything."*

**Matching Modern Work-to-Life Promise:**

*"Helping healthcare professionals build a career of purpose, shaping the future of patient care while advancing their own aspirations."*

## *For a manufacturing company focused on sustainability:*

**Talent Perception:**

*"Judging by their events and content, this company seems to take sustainability seriously, not just in their products but in the way they support their people and the planet."*

**Matching Modern Work-to-Life Promise:**

*"Empowering people to create meaningful change in a workplace that champions sustainability, innovation, and personal growth."*

## *For a digital marketing agency prioritizing creativity and personal growth:*

**Talent Perception:**

*"Their social media posts make it look like a vibrant, creative place where people are encouraged to bring bold ideas to life."*

**Matching Modern Work-to-Life Promise:**

*"Helping marketing professionals find their creative edge and grow as leaders in a dynamic, supportive environment."*

## *For a consultancy focused on leadership development and impact:*

**Talent Perception:**

*"From their thought leadership posts, I get the impression they're deeply committed to developing world-class leaders who make a meaningful impact in their industries."*

**Matching Modern Work-to-Life Promise:**

*"Inspiring professionals to grow into transformative leaders, shaping industries and building a better tomorrow."*

# How to Build Your Desired Employer Brand Perceptions

### 1. Start with Research:

Understand your target audience's motivations and needs. Conduct workshops with current employees, focus groups, or surveys to gather insights about what people value in your organization and what sets you apart from competitors.

### 2. Match Perceptions to Organizational Truths:

Align your desired perceptions with your culture, leadership style, and employee experiences. Don't promise what you can't deliver. Focus on how your existing employees, managers, candidates, subcontractors, and consultants truly experience your culture, values, and collaboration.

**3. Write Your Perceptions from the Talent's Viewpoint:**

Avoid corporate jargon and "we" statements. Think about how someone outside your organization would describe their impressions after interacting with your brand.

**4. Test and Adjust Over Time:**

Employer branding is an iterative process. Periodically check if the perceptions you're projecting align with what your audience feels, and adjust your messaging as needed.

# The Ideal Number of Desired Employer Brand Perceptions

When defining your desired employer brand perceptions, it's crucial to focus on a select few key perceptions. Research by cognitive psychologist George A. Miller suggests that short-term memory can hold approximately seven items, plus or minus two.

However, more recent studies indicate that this capacity may be closer to four chunks of information. This limitation underscores the importance of concentrating on a manageable number of brand perceptions to ensure your organization has the resources to effectively and systematically build on those desired perceptions and ensure your audience will also remember you.

By honing in on three to four core perceptions, you can allocate sufficient resources to each, ensuring consistent and impactful messaging. This approach allows your target audience to recognize and internalize these aspects of your brand, leading to a more authentic and memorable employer image. Attempting to convey too many perceptions can dilute your message and overwhelm your audience, making it harder for any single perception to resonate. Therefore, a focused strategy not only aligns with cognitive processing capabilities but also enhances the clarity and strength of your employer brand.

## Differentiating from Competitors

In employer branding, your competition isn't who sells the same products or services—it's who's vying for the same talent. These employers may be in different industries but match your career opportunities, benefits, ways of work, and leadership style. Identifying and analyzing these competitors is crucial to crafting perceptions that stand out.

## *How to Identify Competitors for Talent*

1.  **Start with Industry Peers:** List companies in your sector hiring for similar roles.
2.  **Expand Beyond Your Industry:** Consider other sectors or companies targeting the same skills, attitudes, and aptitudes.
3.  **Focus on Size and Culture:** Look at organizations that align with your company's size or cultural style, as these factors often influence employee preferences.

Once you've identified your competitors, evaluate their employer branding efforts. What perceptions do they communicate? What's working? What's falling flat?

## *Key Exercise: The Differentiation Workshop*

Bring together employees from your strategic target audience for a workshop. Analyze competitor employer brands to uncover their strengths and gaps. Then, focus on how your organization is different and uniquely positioned to deliver value to the same talent audience.

Ask:

- What sets us apart from these competitors?
- What can we offer that they cannot?
- What would make someone choose us over them?

Differentiation isn't just about being unique—it's about being uniquely relevant to your audience.

## CHAPTER 9

# Key Story Themes: Turning Perceptions into Actionable Content

*"Your brand is what people say about you when you're not in the room."*

JEFF BEZOS

N ow that your desired employer brand perceptions are locked in, it's time to move from intention to execution. This is where Key Story Themes come in. Think of these themes as the foundation for all your employer brand content. They're not just talking points—they're the strategic buckets from which endless content ideas flow.

## Why Key Story Themes Matter

Your Key Story Themes bring your desired employer brand perceptions to life. They connect the dots between what you want to be known for and the real, relatable stories your audience consumes. This is critical because perceptions don't happen in a vacuum—they're built through repeated, consistent, and meaningful messaging. If your target audience consistently encounters stories that align with your Key Story Themes, they'll begin to associate those perceptions with your brand.

Without this focus, your messaging risks becoming diluted. A scattered approach will confuse your audience, delaying or preventing your desired employer brand perceptions from taking root.

## *The Two Equally Important Perspectives of Key Story Themes*

For a truly Magnetic Employer Brand, your Key Story Themes must reflect two distinct perspectives:

## 1. The Company Perspective

This represents the company and focuses on elaborating and demonstrating the business's strategic emphasis, ethos, mission, purpose, values, and organizational culture. It's the "official voice" of your employer brand, ensuring alignment with your company's business goals and building a picture of who your "organization person" is.

Think of the company perspective as the story guide casting an exciting vision, paving the way forward and sharing information, inspiration, and education that helps the hero-talent recognize alignment and build trust in your company as the employer.

## 2. The Employee Perspective

The employee perspective is the voice of employees sharing real-life employee experiences, stories, testimonials, and even insights such as tips, demos, and professional knowledge contributing to the growth of target audience understanding of what the level and depth of knowledge and experience in this organization is.

This behind-the-job-scenes content validates and brings credibility to the company's perspective. The magic happens when these two perspectives work together. The company perspective creates the "what" and "why," while the employee perspective delivers the emotional resonance and trust-building "how" and "how it feels."

## Crafting Your Key Story Themes

Key Story Themes must directly stem from your desired employer brand perceptions; otherwise, the connection between what you post and communicate and what you want your target audience to think about your company disconnects.

Each of your desired employer brand perceptions needs one Key Story Theme to connect the perception with content and communication.

Let's revisit an example:

**Desired Perception:**

"This company appears to be a trailblazer in clean energy solutions, empowering professionals to make a tangible impact on global sustainability."

Examples of Matching Key Story Themes and Content Angles (you would only choose one Key Story Theme per desired perception):

## *Driving the Clean Energy Revolution*

**Examples of the Company Perspective:**

- How sustainable energy aligns with our company mission, vision, and purpose.
- Our values guiding us, keeping our focus and attention on driving the clean energy revolution.

- Why is it so important to us, our clients, stakeholders, and the society?
- What is the latest research, insight, and studies on the topic (our own and those of others)?
- How do we innovate sustainable energy solutions through cutting-edge technology?
- Our company culture and leadership principles driving clean energy revolution.
- Our strategic emphasis on clean energy revolution.

**Examples of Employee Perspective and Experiences:**

- How our people connect with this ethos.
- Examples of insight and experiences driving this ethos.
- How the values and beliefs of our people connect with this ethos.
- Examples of career stories linked to this ethos.
- People stories working directly with this ethos.
- Behind-the-scenes content on witnessing successful outcomes working for the clean energy revolution.
- Thought-leader insights and educational content on the topic.
- Behind-the-scenes content from events and seminars on the topic.

# *Empowering Professional Growth*

## Examples of the Company Perspective:

- How our commitment to professional growth aligns with our company mission, vision, and purpose.

- Our strategic emphasis on fostering a culture of continuous learning and development.

- The role of our leadership principles in creating growth opportunities for all employees.

- Why empowering growth matters to us, our clients, and the industry we serve.

- The innovative programs and initiatives we've developed to fast-track employee career growth.

- Insights and data showcasing the success of our growth-focused culture (e.g., promotions, certifications earned, leadership development participation rates).

- Partnerships with academic institutions, industry organizations, or professional networks to enhance employee skills.

- How our company culture supports experimentation, innovation, and taking calculated risks for personal and professional growth.

**Examples of Employee Perspective and Experiences:**

- Real stories of employees who've grown their careers quickly within our company (e.g., starting as an intern and becoming a manager in three years).

- Testimonials about how employees feel supported in pursuing certifications, degrees, or skill development.

- Examples of employees transitioning into new roles or departments to broaden their expertise.

- Behind-the-scenes stories of mentoring relationships and the impact they've had.

- Employee insights on how leadership has encouraged and enabled their professional development.

- Snapshots of internal workshops, training sessions, or growth programs in action.

- Personal stories about how skills learned here have improved employees' lives outside of work (e.g., financial literacy workshops, public speaking skills).

- Thought-leader insights and advice shared by employees who've grown into industry-recognized professionals.

# Creating Tangible Impact on Sustainability

**Examples of the Company Perspective:**

- How sustainability aligns with our mission, vision, and purpose as a company.
- The specific goals and commitments our organization has made toward sustainability.
- The measurable impact of our sustainability initiatives on the environment and communities we serve.
- How our leadership culture prioritizes sustainability in decision-making.
- The role our products, services, or solutions play in driving sustainability in our industry.
- Partnerships with environmental organizations, NGOs, or research institutions to amplify our impact.
- Case studies of successful sustainability projects or innovations we've delivered.
- The economic and social benefits of our sustainability practices for our stakeholders.

**Examples of Employee Perspective and Experiences:**

- Personal stories of employees who are passionate about sustainability and how they contribute to the cause through their work.
- "Day in the life" narratives from teams working on sustainability projects (e.g., engineers designing energy-efficient solutions).

- Behind-the-scenes stories of fieldwork, testing, or implementation of sustainable initiatives.

- Employee testimonials on how the company supports and inspires their sustainability efforts.

- Stories of employees collaborating with external stakeholders (e.g., community groups, universities) to drive sustainability.

- Insights from employees on how sustainability principles influence daily work and decision-making.

- Visuals and narratives showcasing outcomes of sustainability projects, such as restored habitats, reduced waste, or energy savings.

- Highlights of employees attending or speaking at sustainability-focused events or conferences.

## How to Ideate Endless Content from Key Story Themes

Here's the secret sauce: Key Story Themes are evergreen. They are the lifeblood of your employer brand communication—they're not just talking points; they're dynamic content ecosystems that evolve as your business grows, your employees advance, and your initiatives expand.

When crafted thoughtfully, each theme becomes a wellspring of inspiration, with subtopics and narratives that evolve with your organization. Here's how to ideate content endlessly from your Key Story Themes:

## 1. Break Down the Themes into Angles

Think of each Key Story Theme as a rich narrative. Break it down into:

- **Strategic Angles:** Align with the company's mission, vision, and values.
- **Employee Experiences:** Highlight real stories from your people.
- **Audience Perspectives:** Speak directly to what your target talents care about. For example, if your Key Story Theme is empowering growth, you can create content about:
    - Career development programs.
    - Leadership initiatives and employee growth stories.
    - Workshops, mentorship, and peer learning opportunities.

## 2. Use the Two-Perspective Rule

For every piece of content, ensure you balance:

- The Company Perspective (why these matter to your organization).
- The Employee Perspective (how these play out in real-life employee stories). This dual approach makes your storytelling authentic, relatable, and engaging.

## 3. Adapt to Formats and Platforms

Transform your Key Story Themes into:

- Blog posts and articles.
- Social media updates.
- Behind-the-scenes videos.
- Employee testimonials and podcasts.
- Infographics and white papers.

Every format amplifies the same message differently, increasing reach and resonance.

## 4. Collaborate with Employees

Your employees are the best content creators for your Key Story Themes. Capture their voices through:

- Interviews for articles based on their insight, knowledge, and experiences.
- Case studies.
- Hero Career Stories™. (Check out the Sources, References, and Resources section for available resources on this.)
- Blog posts, video and social media content created by them.

Encourage them to share their authentic perspectives, ensuring the content resonates with both internal and external audiences.

### 5. Leverage Current Trends

Keep your themes fresh and relevant by tying them to current events, industry trends, or societal movements. Remember, you can curate content from other reliable sources and media that share your values and ethos. For example, if sustainability is a Key Story Theme, connect it to global climate action days or innovation in renewable energy.

## Facilitating Key Story Theme Workshops

To ensure your content is rich and varied, consider hosting content ideation workshops. Invite employees who align with your strategic target segments to participate. Here's how to make these sessions impactful:

### 1. Set Clear Goals

Ensure participants understand the purpose of the workshop: to generate subtopics, identify relatable stories, and align on how the themes represent your employer brand.

### 2. Create a Safe and Inclusive Environment

Invite employees from diverse roles, departments, and tenures. Encourage them to share freely without fear of judgment, as the richness of your themes depends on a wide variety of perspectives.

### 3. Use Structured Exercises

- **Storytelling Brainstorm:** Ask employees to share personal anecdotes related to each Key Story Theme.

- **Audience Mapping:** Identify what different talent segments care about most regarding these themes.

- **Content Ideation:** Brainstorm formats for presenting the stories—videos, blogs, live events, etc.

### 4. Incorporate Visual and Interactive Elements

Use tools like whiteboards, sticky notes, or digital collaboration platforms. Create group activities to spark creativity and ensure every voice is heard.

### 5. Document Outcomes

Capture all ideas systematically. Categorize them under the respective Key Story Themes and prioritize based on alignment with desired employer brand perceptions.

## Staying On Brand: Bridging Employer and Company Branding

Branding is a discipline that demands precision, consistency, and an unwavering commitment to staying on message. It's about shaping perceptions and building trust through clarity. For employer branding, this is no different—but it does come with its own unique nuances. I want to clarify not only the importance of staying on brand in employer branding but also how this discipline complements, rather than competes with, the company's master brand.

## The Employer Brand: A Sibling, Not a Twin

Think of the company brand and the employer brand as two siblings raised by the same parents. They share the same values, principles, and overarching purpose—but they are distinct individuals with their own personalities, priorities, and audiences. The company brand appeals to customers, investors, and business partners, focusing on why the organization exists, what it offers, and how it solves problems in the market.

The employer brand, however, speaks to a different audience: the people who already work in the organization and those who might consider joining the company one day. These individuals are not looking at the organization as a buyer would. They're assessing it as a potential home for their career and professional aspirations. They're asking, "Will I grow here? Will I belong here? Will this company make my life better today and tomorrow?"

Even when there's overlap in target audiences—such as B2B experts who could be both customers and potential employees—their decision-making processes are fundamentally different. A customer assesses the company with their professional role in mind, often considering ROI for their employer. But when the same individual evaluates the company as an employer, their criteria shift to personal growth, workplace culture, and alignment with their own values. This is why the employer brand is not a carbon copy of the company brand. It's a sibling—distinct but aligned.

## Why Staying on Brand Matters for Both

For those in marketing, the idea of "staying on brand" is second nature. Every message, visual, and interaction is carefully calibrated to reinforce the company's core identity. In employer branding, this principle is equally vital. When HR and talent acquisition teams stray from the company's brand voice, tone, or core values, they risk creating confusion and mistrust among audiences. A disjointed message—where the employer brand feels like a separate entity—undermines credibility for both brands.

This doesn't mean that employer branding teams should mimic marketing campaigns word for word. Instead, they must craft messages that reflect the company's essence while tailoring the story with its visuals to resonate with talent. It's about creating a seamless experience that feels authentic, whether someone encounters your brand as a customer or as a potential employee.

Here's the key: Employer branding must interpret the company brand for the talent audience. It must tell the same story but in a way that feels personal, relevant, and human to those evaluating you as a workplace. This is where alignment and differentiation go hand in hand.

## *Collaborating for Brand Success*

Marketing professionals, I want to acknowledge your expertise and the critical role you play in protecting and evolving the company brand. As a seasoned marketing communications professional, I deeply respect the art and science of branding. That's why employer branding strategies in The Magnetic Employer Branding Method™ are designed to integrate seamlessly with your branding efforts—not compete with them. However, having worked for a decade in HR development and talent acquisition, I also know how vital it is for the employer brand to resonate with existing and future employees from the angle that is only relevant in the context of career, professional development, and work-life balance.

Here's how this methodology helps you to stay on brand while ensuring the employer brand serves its unique purpose:

### 1. Shared Values, Shared Story

Both brands share the same foundational elements—values, vision, mission, and purpose. This ensures consistency and credibility across all audiences.

### 2. Tailored Messaging

Employer branding translates the company's broader story into a narrative that resonates with talent. For example, if the company brand emphasizes innovation, the employer brand might highlight how employees drive that innovation through their work and how that work contributes to customer promise.

## 3. Targeted Visuals and Tone

The employer brand may adopt a more conversational and approachable tone compared to the company brand, which might be more formal or polished. The visuals may focus more on people, teams, and experiences rather than products or services.

## 4. Collaborative Content Creation

I believe in working together with marketing and communication to ensure alignment. This includes co-creating guidelines for employer brand visuals, tone, and messaging to maintain coherence with the company brand.

# A Vision for Unified Branding

When employer branding and marketing teams collaborate effectively, the results are transformative. The employer brand becomes a natural extension of the company brand—a vibrant, human expression of what it means to be part of your organization. This synergy deepens trust, not just with talent, but with all stakeholders who see a cohesive and authentic story that resonates across all touchpoints.

Returning to the family analogy: The company brand and employer brand are like two individuals walking in the same direction, guided by the same purpose, but speaking to different audiences along the way. Together, they create a complete and compelling picture of who you are as an organization—both in the marketplace and as an employer.

Key Story Themes act as your guardrails. They ensure that every piece of employer branding content aligns with your strategy and reinforces the perceptions you want to build. By focusing exclusively on themes that seamlessly connect your company's business goals, purpose, and culture with your employees' experiences, you ensure that:

- Your messaging is clear and consistent.
- Your target audience forms the exact perceptions you're aiming for.
- You avoid the trap of random, unaligned posts that dilute your brand's image.

When your employer branding strategy stays on course with these Key Story Themes, your employer brand becomes a magnetic force—pulling in the right people, building loyalty, and strengthening your competitive edge. It's a win for marketing, HR, and, most importantly, for your business's future.

SECTION 3

# THE TALENT JOURNEY: YOUR MAGNETIC COMMUNICATION PROCESS

## CHAPTER 10

# Phase One: Winning Sustainable Attention

*"Learning to persuade is a fundamental life skill most people never take time to learn."*

PROFESSOR ROBERT B. CIALDINI

## The Talent Journey of the Information Era™: Your Magnetic Employer Brand Communication Framework

Winning sustainable attention is the invitation phase of your target talent's journey with your company. Talent Journey refers to the time and the phases a person in your target audience needs to go through before they are ready for the action or change you propose to them.

Getting attention used to be a default, but we lost this privilege more than a decade ago. Memorize this: You no longer automatically have the attention of your target audiences. Your company doesn't have it. To win the attention, even just once, requires way more work and luck than ten or twenty years ago, or even just five years ago!

Campaigns are meant to win the attention for a short period of time. When you need to win attention again, you must run another campaign. With each campaign, you compete with millions of other campaigns chasing the same attention at the same time.

Are you sure your campaign is compelling enough to win this auction of limited attention? The likelihood is that it isn't unless you are prepared to make it bigger, bolder, and louder than the competition, but you don't know what the competition is doing until you see it yourself, and it's going to be too late for your company to enter the same competition at that point.

The problem is that you cannot win sustainable attention with a one-off campaign. If you are lucky and win the attention, you win it only as long as your campaign is active. When it ends, attention is gone to some other company's campaign. What if you didn't have to repeat the huge effort each separate campaign requires? What if you could create a more lasting impact with much less effort and strain instead?

Short-and-sassy campaigns work well in recruiting, where you need job seekers to react and send their applications quickly. What you offer in recruiting is immediate value in return for attention in the form of a recruitment process and relatively quick resolution. However, in employer branding, you don't have anything that quick and fast to offer because your passive target audience doesn't have the same sense of urgency to act.

So, what are you campaigning about in employer branding? A bold-and-loud employer branding campaign for a week or two doesn't mean a thing apart from making a huge dent in your budget. The impact is next to none, very different from recruitment campaigns. In fact, I don't know any business in this universe with a big enough employer branding budget to keep doing bold-and-loud campaigns often enough to achieve the transitions from stage to stage the Talent Journey requires.

We communicate to our current and future employees all the time, but is it effective? Does your message get through to them? After they see your message, do they take the action you wanted, expected, or even asked for?

Sometimes, you see organizations pull off a proper extravaganza to win the attention of their target audience. Career events make a great example. Those certainly win attention but also cost a tall penny. For an extravaganza to turn into sustainable attention and actual value for your organization, you need a plan and a budget for what to do with that attention after the event is over and your extravaganza is stored in a cardboard box. Otherwise, you paid a lot for the event, people had fun, but you don't know if there will be any return on the investment (ROI).

We all know what the top management thinks about adding more costs if there is an uncertainty of what value they get in return. While extravaganzas can be excellent in winning attention, if all the effort (and budget) is invested in a one activity or step, you can forget about the candidate's journey to value-added conversions.

The Magnetic Employer Branding Method™ provides you with a communication framework for an ongoing employer brand communication that spreads your employer branding efforts over a longer period, persuading relevant talents to find an emotional connection with your company and become likelier to choose you as their employer in their next career step.

Instead of putting all your resources, energy, and effort into a one-off activity to win attention, in this methodology, the first phase of winning sustainable attention seamlessly integrates with growing employer awareness, building employer brand affinity, and finally, converting employer brand value back to your business. How long this journey lasts is different for each individual on this journey with your company, but once they are at the end of the journey, they will choose your company. That is the power of The Magnetic Employer Branding Method™.

## Winning Sustainable Attention

Why does attention matter? Winning your target audience's attention means they become consciously aware of your employer brand messages. They notice if you post or publish something and give it that vital second or two of their attention to decide whether it is something they should check out. If your content reciprocates their effort, they are more likely to pay attention to your message the next time you post. This is because the algorithm picked up that they spent time on your post, so the algorithm is more likely to push your next post on their feeds. However, failure to make your next post equally valuable and resonant will likely lead them to skip your content. When the algorithm picks this up, it will replace your posts in your target audience's feeds with someone else's posts.

Unfortunately, many companies continue to mistakenly believe their audiences see everything they post. LinkedIn, being the most popular social media platform for recruitment marketing and employer branding, made significant changes to its algorithm in October 2023. The most noticeable impact was a huge decrease on how many followers see our company posts.

With this change, posts from personal profiles are shown to 10 percent of our followers. If you thought this is quite a small portion, posts from company profiles are only shown to 2 percent of the followers!

If your company has 1,000 followers on LinkedIn, each post is only shown to twenty of your followers. These twenty followers are chosen by the algorithm based on their interaction with your company's LinkedIn profile and previous posts. Your company's followers on LinkedIn are likely to be a mix of employees, customers, salespeople, stakeholders such as investors, media and other relevant public entities, and then, job seekers interested in your company. How many of those twenty people are your relevant employer branding audience? Getting attention on LinkedIn became hard in October 2023!

LinkedIn is not the reason why winning attention is so hard. Decreasing attention is the product of the digital age. And it is no wonder. Every minute of every day, at least half a million new comments are posted on Facebook, at least 350,000 tweets are being sent, at least 21 million snaps are being created, 210 million emails and 15 million texts are sent. We watch at least 700 videos on TikTok every minute of every day, while you folks in the US alone also stream 694 million songs at the same time! These are just some examples of what happens online every sixty seconds. How will you get your employer branding message into the top selection of your target audience? It's a busy place, the Internet, and so are the minds of our target audience.

Can you now see why winning sustainable attention matters? Without sustaining the attention of your employer brand's target audience, you have to work so much harder to win it over and over again from scratch. If all your efforts and resources go into recreating attention, your attempt to build employer awareness, grow employer brand affinity, and convert value from employer branding will fail—because you are not doing any actions to win them. Learning to win sustainable attention is the key to creating an employer brand that lasts the test of time. And I wouldn't count on LinkedIn's help on this.

## Winning Sustainable Attention is a Cognitive Process

Attention refers to the cognitive process of focusing on a particular stimulus or information. It allows us to selectively concentrate on one aspect of our environment while ignoring others. In today's fast-paced world filled with distractions, capturing and maintaining attention is crucial, whether in personal interactions, marketing, education, or other aspects of life. "Sustainable attention" extends this concept further. It refers to the ability to maintain someone's focus over time in an effective but also ethical and respectful way.

In marketing and communications, sustainable attention involves engaging with your audience in a manner that adds genuine value, fosters trust, and builds long-term relationships. Instead of resorting to attention-grabbing advertising tactics that are often short-lived, sustainable attention focuses on creating meaningful connections and providing valuable content or experiences. For example, in employer branding, sustainable attention might involve consistently sharing educational information or using business storytelling to inspire and even teach something meaningful to your target audience. By doing so, you capture attention and maintain it by fostering a genuine connection with your audience.

Sustainable attention is about nurturing relationships and loyalty, rather than just seeking fleeting moments of engagement. It's an approach that values integrity, empathy, and long-term sustainability in building and maintaining attention. Your first Magnetic Employer Branding goal with this methodology is to win sustainable attention that sticks. In social media terms, we could say that one-time attention does not turn a person in the audience into your follower. Sustainable attention means your audience grows as you reach the attention of the same people more than once; they like what they see and "subscribe" to see more by becoming followers. In a world where attention is no longer a default, winning sustainable attention is a critical step in successfully becoming a Magnetic Employer.

## How our Brain Works to Keep us Alive and Why it Matters in Employer Branding

Thanks to our brains, humans have a natural resistance to change. Our brain has been programmed to alarm us when the current conditions are changing, and we need to be wary of this pending change because we don't know whether the change is dangerous or safe. Losing our control in a changing circumstance makes us stressed and anxious. It is not because we object to change as such, but because of the uncertainty of not knowing what happens and how the change impacts us. Because of this, we prefer to keep things as they are until we can be sure the change brings us something better than what we have now.

As babies, we go through a period when we shun unfamiliar people. It is the same primal instinct: Our brain teaches us not to trust a stranger because it could be dangerous, automatically. As employees, we find change difficult when we are not prepared for it early enough, and we don't get the information we need to help us see how the approaching change impacts us.

Usually, management has way more time to make themselves comfortable and control the change before the staff is informed about it. And when the staff becomes alarmed and stressed, the management no longer understands it because they know everything about the change and control it. So, the employees' resistance annoyed the management when all they needed to do was start communicating the change much earlier.

What about physical events? The next time you go to a physical event such as a seminar, a course, or an after-work event, and you meet unfamiliar people, watch yourself positioning yourself near the exit and at the back of the room. Most people do this. We behave like this because our brain tells us to stay near the exit, just in case the event isn't safe. Safe in this case means exciting and relevant for us to stick around. Our brain functions the same way despite the dangers are no longer predators of the wild but predators of technology and irrelevant information.

The key difference between employer branding and recruitment campaigns is that urgency of the target person to act. When a job seeker is actively looking for a job, they are urgently paying attention to relevant job posts and offers. This is when their brain organizes recruitment messages and marketing into the container of "relevant information." It is easier to get active job seekers to notice your recruitment campaign because of the urgency in their minds when receiving recruitment information. Employer branding messages are not recruitment messages, and your target audience has no urgency to pay attention to your employer branding messages unless their brain organizes those messages into the same relevant information container.

Now, you may think, *Why should I build an employer brand if employer branding is irrelevant to job seekers?* And that is a wonderful question I've been waiting to answer!

Think about all the open vacancies populating job boards. How does your target audience member end up finding yours? Is your target audience member even in a state of urgency to find a new job when you are hiring?

To make this simple, let's say your relevant talent is in an urgency to find a new job when you are hiring because they are either currently unemployed or graduating very soon and need a job. Urgency confirmed. Next, how do they find your vacancy when there are hundreds, if not hundreds of thousands, of vacancies available?

Simple classification. They use criteria such as the industry, type of role, experience required, salary, and location. Now, their list is much shorter. But usually long enough not to have time to go through every vacancy open right now.

Guess where they start? With employers they know and trust—employers who have a brand.

They now quickly scan through job posts of employers with perceived trust and appeal to understand whether the role seems interesting or not. Depending on how much time they have available—their own and the deadline for the application—they proceed with only those opportunities that appear interesting and match with their timeline.

This consideration process is where your employer brand matters because the less they know about your organization, the more risk your company and offer possess in their eyes. Humans are simply much more likely to proceed with options they feel they can trust and that hold value beyond the pay and benefits. This is the value of having a Magnetic Employer Brand. You are chosen before others.

## Relevant Employers Win Sustainable Attention

Relevancy is always in the eyes of the beholder. What makes you relevant to the people you want to hire and retain is based on what matters to them, not what matters to you as the employer, and especially not to those who create employer branding content and messages.

The key to becoming relevant is making your employer brand about your target audience, not about you. Your employer brand value is not the value you expect to be gained but the value that ties your target audience emotionally with your

STORY-DRIVEN EMPLOYER BRANDING

brand. As a result, your company starts to receive business-worthy value from employer branding.

But your employer brand's content and messages must communicate value-add for the audience, not what you expect from them. When you convince your target audience that you as their employer can help them transform their lives for the better to match what they seek, need, or aspire to, you become a relevant employer and win their sustainable attention as long as you continue to make them believe that. And this is all down to how good of a communicator you are.

## Great communicators all share three key characteristics:

1. **They are understood**. They know how to articulate their thoughts or ideas into a clear message.
2. **They are interesting**. They have the skill to win attention and captivate their audience with their message.
3. **They inspire change**. A message that fails to change the recipient's attitudes, beliefs, or behavior is a failed message.

The Talent Journey of the Information Era™ is the communication framework for your employer brand communication process that I recommend you follow, both in your internal and external talent communication, if you want your messages to truly convince and convert.

149

You can boost the impact of your message with acts of planned marketing, such as advertising, broadcasting, sharing, promoting, and asking others to advocate your message. But unless you understand that the action you desire from your audience is at the end of this journey, and that there are many "barriers" for you to cross before your target audience makes it to the end of their respective journeys with your company, your messages are likely to fail.

There are four phases of the Talent Journey of the Information Era™ starting with winning sustainable attention and ending in value conversions that deliver the expected return on the employer branding investment. This journey isn't linear. In fact, it is more of a wheel that turns into a funnel. You constantly need new people jumping in this wheel, and this is where the wheel is widest, like the top of a funnel. You will notice over time some people jump out of the wheel while others pause because what you communicate, and post, is not relevant for them at that time. Or, because your messages and marketing fail to win *sustainable* attention and move them forward on this journey. Oftentimes, other people and companies win their attention, and they exit this journey to enter a competing one.

If you think about your employer branding goals (explained in Chapter 5), you recognize the phases on the Talent Journey are the same. I designed this on purpose to tie your employer brand communication process with what success needs to look like during each phase. This will help you to align your employer brand communication goals with your employer brand marketing actions.

The science of storytelling is present throughout the Talent Journey in the role reversal: The talent is the hero in your employer branding messages and content, while you as the employer are the guide they can trust to lead them to a better work life. This helps you win sustainable attention and keep your relevant audience members engaged with your company until they are ready to convert. The employer brand affinity phase is where you want to apply business storytelling the most because it is the only form of communication, proven by science, that evokes emotions in the recipient. Persuasive communication tactics should be applied throughout the journey to enhance the impact and influence of your messages. You will learn how as I take you through each of the phases during the next chapters. But let's start with winning sustainable attention.

*Go to section 'What's next? Free Resources That Come with This Book' to download The Talent Journey of the Information Era™ PDF.*

## The Importance of Winning Sustainable Attention

Employer branding is not a campaign like recruitment marketing. The aim of employer branding is not to get applications for a current recruitment process, but to change the way your target audience looks at your company and you as an employer. Permanently. It is paramount to separate employer branding from recruitment campaigns. When you have a Magnetic Employer Brand, your talent acquisition becomes much easier, and you probably need to invest much less in recruitment campaigns, but building an employer brand does not take place in your recruitment marketing collateral. Your target talents are already at the value conversions phase of their Talent Journeys with your company when they convert as job applicants. The employer branding part takes place much earlier and begins with winning sustainable attention.

Why sustainable? Because starting with winning attention repeatedly keeps your target audience at the beginning of this Talent Journey, and they never move forward. It costs you much more in your employer branding budget, time, and other resources if they never move forward on their Talent Journey with your company specifically. It is like dating. You keep meeting different people, but you never move past the first date with anyone, and the idea of finding your partner isn't getting any closer.

Instead, when your goal is to win sustainable attention, your "organization person's relationship" with your target audience members develops and moves forward, creating value for both parties.

## The First Phase is an Invitation Phase on a Loop

Consider winning sustainable attention as the invitation phase. What this means is that you must keep those invites always going out. Remember, this is not a campaign where you post once to announce an opening, but more like a profile on a dating app that stays active. It is equivalent to you showing up regularly at the spots where single people mingle. Instead of just one nightclub, your "organization person" is socially active and regularly present to remind the target audience about their existence as well as engaging in conversations with the aim to attract like-minded people.

In practice, this is your company's regular social media presence in one or more platforms where your target audience is likely to hang out and socialize with their peers regularly. Your "organization person" has a profile, preferably dedicated to employer branding and talent acquisition.

This first phase on the Talent Journey introduces and invites your target audience to start paying attention to your content and messages, with the goal of them becoming followers. They are unlikely to start following you immediately, but as they keep "bumping into you," they will—if they like the vibe of your "organization person."

Appearing very human in your posts and content will accelerate the process of converting into followers. This is the first rule of winning sustainable attention in employer branding. If you post behind the company logo, never engage in conversations, keep it impersonal, and what's worse, about your company news, you will fail at the start of what could have been a wonderfully inspiring opportunity to build your employer awareness, grow a fantastic reputation, and become a talent magnet.

## How Do You Win Sustainable Attention?

You can only win sustainable attention when your employer branding positions your relevant talent as the hero and your company as their trusted advisor to a better life. These roles come directly from storytelling. This role reversal means every single post, message, and piece of content you create and publish is about the talent, not about your company. Instead of talking about who you are, what you do, and what you need, you take that information, select what is relevant for your target audience, and change the key message into who your target talent is, what they currently do, what they probably want to do and achieve, and how being part of your company will help them to build the life they desire.

When your employer branding messages resonate with your audience and add immediate value, you will be able to win attention at a fraction of the cost that you pay for loud-and-bold campaigns. Immediate value comes in four types: informational, educational, inspirational, and entertaining. All you need to know is what topics are meaningful and valuable for your target people, and when are the best times to approach them with any of these four types of content.

Knowing your audience is vital in winning their sustainable attention. As a former HR professional, I know how much data HR collects and has available. But I also know how little we use this data. Getting to know your target audience starts with becoming interested in them as people and individuals, just like you would if you wanted to become friendly with someone personally. Using the data collected regularly by HR and listening to what your recruiters face daily as they search for, get to know, and interview candidates must become your regular habit. It is impossible to win sustainable attention without knowing what triggers your target audience. And, without attention, the Talent Journey stops before it begins.

**The Magnetic Employer Branding Method™ provides you the following means to help you win sustainable attention:**

**#1 The ongoing Talent Journey communication framework** reminds you of the importance of adopting the habit of regular employer brand communication instead of the occasional campaigns when your company needs talents to act.

**#2 The Master Plan**, where you identified the Key Story Themes. They act as your key talking points throughout your employer branding messages, content, and communication. When you make sure all your posts reflect your Key Story Themes, your relevant and ideal target audience will be able to identify themselves in your narrative and become attracted by your organization on a deeper level than a mere job opportunity. Random posts do not have this impact.

**#3 "The talent is the hero" role reversal** reminds you how you must avoid talking about your company's needs and wants, or what you or other people inside your company think is interesting about your company. Instead, you need to invest a little bit of your organization's resources into regularly engaging with your target audience on social media to learn what they think is interesting.

This isn't anything more demanding than having someone or collectively some people regularly following and engaging with your target audience to see what topics they post about or comment on and in what tone. Additionally, you can invest in social listening tools and keyword search tools, but it would be best if your "organization's person" showed up regularly for your followers.

**#4 You are the employer they learn to see as their trusted guide.** Adopting this role, from the value and topics you provide in your content to the tone of voice and style of communication, turns you into an interesting and valuable source of information to your target talent audiences. While you want to be recognizable as an employer to all your company's stakeholders and not appear completely different from your company's brand (not any product or service brand but company brand, if you have one), it is vital to remember that you are branding a different side of your company to a different target audience.

Your company's customers, investors, and other stakeholders have different needs and expectations toward your company and business, and your company's commercial brand should resonate with those. But just like your employer brand is unlikely to get customers to make a purchase, your company's commercial brand is unlikely to get your target talents to see themselves building a better life as part of your company. Your commercial and employer brand are like loyal partners in marriage or siblings in the same family with shared vision, goals, and values for life, but they are independent characters in the same success story.

**#5 The pillars in the content plan** explained in the next section will guide you on what type of content and messages have the greatest impact when applied in your employer branding content. When you follow the content plan according to this methodology, you can't help but sustain your target audience's attention and convince and convert your relevant and ideal talents to keep moving forward on their Talent Journeys with your organization until the time is right for both parties to make the commitment of employment.

**#6 The application of storytelling and persuasion in your content and communication.** When you regularly make your content and messages about your target audience, not about what your company wants or needs, you are automatically more likely to win their sustainable attention even if you have no idea how to write stories. In the next pages, I will give you more detailed examples and information about applying the science of storytelling and persuasion in your employer branding content and messages.

## A Narrative Communication Formula

There is a universal structure to a story called the dramatic arc. A story always has certain characters with specific roles in the story. The hero character has a problem, and the pain caused by that problem gets harder until the hero realizes they cannot get rid of this pain alone. Here comes a guide who offers them a plan. The guide casts a vision of a positive outcome if the hero follows the plan provided by the guide. The problem gets bigger if the hero chooses not to follow the plan. In a story, the guide is always positioned as an empathetic authority with plenty of experience with what the hero is going through. At the end of the story, the hero wins the day, and at that moment, they become the hero. *What this means is that the hero is an aspiring hero when the story begins, and they only become the hero with the help of the guide.* The guide has a critical role in the success of the aspiring hero-person. The aspiring hero character must win the day; otherwise, something awful takes place. In a movie, usually someone they love dies. In real-life work, that of course isn't the case, but we all have experienced very painful elements that have hindered our career development or mental well-being that needed to be solved.

Learning to apply the science of storytelling can take some time, as, unfortunately, our brains are not hardwired to automatically tell stories like they are to understand stories. That's why I want to share with you a simple narrative-based communication formula I have learned from Donald Miller's work. You can apply this narrative formula in all your content, from social media and blog posts to job posts and employer branding video content. It gives you a simple storytelling formula that you can use without having to insert yourself heavily in the science of storytelling.

## #1 Identifying the problem

A narrative content starts with identifying the problem the target person is likely to have. This acts as an attention hook, making it immediately obvious for the *relevant* viewer to recognize your content is something they absolutely need to check out. How I teach this to our clients and coaching students is to practice this on social media posts. Write the post first, just as you intended. Then, take the ending sentence or paragraph and bring it to the beginning of the copy text. Usually, we leave the beef at the end, but you always want to start with it.

Adjust the beginning sentence to frame the problem in a way that feels urgent and personal. For example, if your last sentence says, *"If you're feeling stuck applying for countless jobs but not getting any responses…"* simply adjust it, for example, like this: *"Feeling stuck applying for countless jobs but never hearing back?"* This directly addresses a common frustration job seekers face, hooking their attention by speaking to their struggle and making them want to read on to find the solution your post proposes to them.

When you start your message with the problem your target audience member can identify with, you immediately pull in the attention of anyone experiencing this issue. The goal is to lead with the pain point or desire that your audience feels so they instantly see themselves in your post and feel compelled to keep reading. Remember, it's all about showing them that you understand their struggle and that you have the solution they're looking for. This way, you are positioning yourself as the guide.

I want to clarify here, that even though I gave you a recruitment-related example, as an employer branding post, this would not be about your open vacancy and a call to action to send their application. In employer branding, you are simply using this as an example to win attention and tie the message to your company culture and values. You could use this line as a hook to talk about how your organization gives and receives feedback and makes timely attempts to respond to all internal and external messages within a specific time frame.

**#2 Making the problem feel worse**

Next, you must agitate the problem to amplify the emotional resonance and urgency of the issue, as this makes the relevant reader feel seen and understood. This is a very important element in all storytelling. When you highlight the frustration, disappointment, or anxiety associated with their problem—like feeling ignored after applying for jobs or struggling to stand out despite their skills—you create an emotional connection where you further position your company as a guide that can help your target audience build a better life. I know it might seem odd in business communication to agitate a problem, but I guarantee you this approach triggers a response where they not only recognize the issue but feel compelled to hear your solution. Why this works so well is because it knocks on the door of the emotions chamber, making the problem feel real and immediate for the audience.

Those who recognize the struggle feel motivated to keep reading and engage with your content, as it promises to address their pain. People often ask me: "How do I find my target audience members on social media other than LinkedIn?" This is how you find your ideal and relevant target audience members. Also, on LinkedIn, a job title doesn't mean they are your ideal and relevant target audience. When you agitate the problem your organization's culture, values, ethics, beliefs, and opportunities can fix, those people who identify with the problem are relevant people in your employer branding audience.

Here is an example of what agitating the problem looks like (bold parts) in our example post:

*"**Feeling stuck** applying for countless jobs but **never hearing back**? It's **frustrating**, isn't it? **You spend hours** perfecting your CV, tailoring each application, and hitting 'send'—**only to be met with silence. The uncertainty** of not knowing what you're **doing wrong** can make you **question your** skills and your worth. It feels like you're shouting into the void, **hoping for** a response that **never comes**. But what if there's a way to change that?"*

All the words written in bold express agitated problems. By emphasizing the emotional toll—frustration, uncertainty, and self-doubt—you intensify the reader's pain point, making them feel understood and ready to engage with the solution you're about to present.

### #3 Telling them how the problem gets solved

Now that your relevant reader is emotionally charged with the problem, they want to hear how you can help them change it. This is where you step up in the role of the guide, providing them an actionable tip or two they can use immediately. Let's look at how this post might continue:

*"First, when you apply for a role, follow up with a polite message a week later. It shows initiative and reminds the recruiter of your application without coming across as pushy. Second, use LinkedIn to connect with someone in the company—maybe a recruiter, hiring manager for the role, or even a team member in the department you applied to. Express your enthusiasm for the role and how you're keen to understand more about the company culture.*

*"But here's the key: While you're taking these steps to stand out, pay attention to how they (as the representatives of the company) respond. If the recruiter or the hiring manager is silent or vague, it might be a sign that communication isn't a priority in their culture, or their culture doesn't hold much value for their employees and candidates. Great companies value transparency and timely communication because they understand that building relationships starts at the first touchpoint.*

*"This is your opportunity to reflect on whether their values align with what you're seeking in a workplace. After all, the hiring process often mirrors what it's like to work there—if they respect and engage with you now, it's a strong indicator that they'll do the same once you're part of the team."*

How does this make you feel as a reader? This is an example of an employer branding post. It's not about your current vacancy, but how your company would behave and treat their candidates and how that behavior translates to your company's values and culture. Of course, these would have to be a true reflection of your culture, values, and likely candidate experiences in your company's case.

## #4 Talking about what life looks like once their problem is solved

Once you, as the guide, have provided your reader, the hero, a solution to their emotionally charged problem, you want to leave them with a curiosity to become more familiar with your organization as a potential workplace. In your post, you next frame what the future is likely to look like for them when they choose employers based on culture and values match. As you frame the vision of their likely future, you describe your own company culture and values to tie this post to your company without making it about you, but about them and what benefits them:

*"Imagine working in a company that values your time and effort from day one—a place where you're met with clear communication, transparency, and respect. When you choose an employer whose culture and values align with yours, the difference is undeniable. You feel valued, empowered, and*

*supported in your growth. Your voice matters, and you're not just another name on a list; you're part of a community that genuinely wants you to succeed.*

*"That's the kind of place where your potential thrives, and your work feels meaningful. The hiring process doesn't need to be your first experience into a company's culture. Get to know potential organizations, like us, through their presence as employers and individuals on social media. Choose wisely—your future self will thank you for it."*

This keeps the post impactful while painting a vivid picture of the reader's potential future when they choose an employer aligned with their values, all while staying concise for social media.

## #5 Call to action to connect with your company

You then finish your post with a call to action to follow your account to learn more about your company's culture and values and what their life could look like if they were working in your organization.

This is as simple as: *"Follow us @ [the handle you want them to follow] to become familiar with the culture, values, and beliefs we hold as an organization, employer, and a community of talents."*

Depending on which social media you would post this, you might have to make it shorter, turn it into a video, or make it a carousel post, taking advantage of both the space on the visual content and the captions.

# How the Science of Persuasion Helps You Win Sustainable Attention

What if there was a way of communicating that made it way more likely to influence another person's attitudes and behavior in ways you desired? Imagine if, just by way of communication, your employer branding and other talent marketing messages persuaded your target audience to pay attention, read through, and take actions favorable to your organization. What would that mean to you in your work and career, your employer's business, the entire organization, and your staff?

The other scientific element providing The Magnetic Employer Branding Method™ a strong foundation is the science of persuasion—*ethical* persuasion. Persuasion means how people influence one another—changing someone's beliefs, decisions, or actions through reasoning or request. The psychology of persuasion can be summarized in the following chain of events, kicking off from the communication with:

- The person pays attention and invests some time to comprehend the message.

- Something in the message impacts the person in ways that make them consider the message and become influenced to agree, believe, and carry out the suggested action.

- The recipient's reaction to the message depends, in part, on the message itself, but to a considerable extent on how they perceive or interpret it.

Two masters of persuasion—best-selling author Daniel H. Pink and professor Robert B. Cialdini—inspired me to start learning about the science behind it. While Professor Cialdini's take on persuasion is very theoretical, Pink's is very practical.

Daniel H. Pink talks about selling, but not in the way you assume. I know this because I also assumed his work to be about hard selling. But it isn't. He calls his perspective the "non-sales selling," and as someone who, as an introvert, has had a fear of approaching strangers and being the conversion starter in a room of unknown people, I was immediately hooked on his work. In particular, this: "We are persuading, convincing, and influencing others to give up something they've got in exchange for what we've got."

- Recruiters sell reasons to choose their vacancies all the time.

- HR professionals persuade management, team leaders, and staff to follow HR policies and practices and pay more attention to improving employee retention and talent acquisition.

- Communication professionals spend most of their time framing information and words into a convincing context.

- Marketers are using multiple channels, platforms, and marketing tools daily to drive customers' desires to consider and purchase.

- Management and team leaders persuade people at the day's end to deliver goals and objectives.

- Whatever your profession is, you present ideas to employees, colleagues, and customers, and make pitches to job seekers and new clients, all the time.

## The Most Essential Lesson in Persuasion

Did you know that one of the most significant obstacles in successful communication and marketing is when we make it about us, our business, and our need to sell? This is equally common in HR marketing. Most job posts communicate only what the hiring employer needs, wants, requests, and expects to be finished by when they want it. But what about the job seeker? Imagine if our sales pitches followed the same "me-me" formula!

They'd be like: "We expect you to buy this from us by then and then. Our request is for the payment to be done on this date. And finally, we need you as the client to have this, this, and that, behave like this, follow these, and master this, that, and the other. What we offer to you is our challenges and nice people to collaborate with who are paid the industry standard pay and benefits."

That's why the most essential lesson in ethical persuasion I can give you is the change of perspective.

I recently had an experience with a new client who has a fantastic company and products. This business operates in an industry that is seriously transforming, and it brings incredible technology to the future of the industry. However, they have a problem. Their target audiences barely know they exist. The HR director asked me to write a persuasive job post for a very challenging role of a senior B2B salesperson. She knew very well the B2B salespeople they want are extremely sought after and can afford to choose only the career opportunities with the least risk and most gain. An unknown employer is a high-risk employer to a job seeker. The more experienced you are as a professional and the more desired candidate you are, the less you need to take unnecessary risks. I'm sure no employer ever considers this, even if they feel the same about candidates who are unknown to them. That's why recruiters vet candidates carefully and check their references thoroughly.

I knew a standard job post would not cut it, so I used ethical persuasion and business storytelling on the job post. The HR director responded that reading the job post had made them cry because it was so appealing. Their CEO liked it, too. But then, the company marketing department was adamant to make changes to it. Guess what they did? They replaced at least half of the persuasive and storytelling elements from the text with standard business information about the company. When I later asked the HR manager how the recruitment went, she had little to say. It is not persuasive when it isn't about the target person.

Promoting "you," your company, products, services, and open jobs, has a minimal impact on your target audience. Promoting how you can help your audience solve some of their biggest pain points has a huge impact on your target audience because when the pain has grown big enough, they haven't been able to solve it by themselves. They are looking for someone who can help them take away that pain.

When you want to influence and persuade others to consider your view, opinion, idea, solution, or organization, changing perspective is at the heart of moving others. Changing perspective means you make your message about them and their needs, not about you and yours. This perspective-taking means stepping in someone else's shoes. In the case of employer branding, those shoes are the shoes of your existing and future employees who are capable, inspired, and willing to turn their potential into the success of your business.

Martin Lorentzon, who co-founded Spotify, has allegedly said that the value of your company is equal to the sum of the problems you can solve. If your company wants to increase its perceived value, it must improve its problem-solving capability.

Neuroscience suggests that taking someone else's perspective is one of the key strategies for it. Not just because it helps us gain information about a complex situation, but because perspective-taking activates brain regions linked with creativity and innovation. These areas in our brains help us understand others and what they want, need, or find important.

No one apart from neuroscientists would remember the names of these parts in our brain, so let's call them the "mentalizing network," chosen by researchers at Washington University in St. Louis. They discovered these areas of the brain activate when we take a break from active problem-solving.

What this means in your ordinary Magnetic Employer Branding activity of creating content is that when you change your perspective from that of your company to that of your target audience, not only will your content influence, persuade, and convince better those who consume it, but you also feel more creative and explorative when you create the content. You must try this, and you will see the difference!

## *Three Principles of Perspective-Taking*

In his book *To Sell is Human*, Daniel H. Pink explains how perspective-taking is based on these three principles:

1. Increasing your power by reducing it.
2. Using your head as much as your heart.
3. Mimicking strategically.

The more experienced someone is and the more miles they have behind them, the more attuned they are to others. Early in my career, I used whatever power I had to compensate for my lack of authority and experience to get my point across. The more experienced I became, the less power I felt I needed to use to deliver my message. Today, I feel almost nonchalant about it because I know how incredibly powerful this methodology is, and I don't feel the need to bend over backward to prove it. But when I started my first business, I found myself vulnerable, doubting, and lacking self-confidence. I needed skills I didn't yet have and was in a very different position and role than today.

With my fear of cold calling, I was often almost paralyzed with anxiety about how strongly I needed to influence potential clients to be the breadwinner for my family. I used complex language and lots of terminology in my sales and marketing efforts, mistakenly believing my target audience would be more attracted by my offer and think more highly of me. I focused on talking about how amazing my services were and how awesome I believed I was as a consultant and employer, thinking I would impress the audience and make them want me over other options.

Focusing on oneself is typical human behavior. I learned the hard way. It is humane to believe the best way to influence others to do what we want them to do is to coerce them with favorable information about us and describe our needs in detail. We position ourselves as the ones with the power, expecting that to be a turn-on when, in fact, it is a massive turn-off.

By increasing your power, Pink means that we shift our focus from ourselves to that of the target audience. This is done by positioning ourselves as the ones with less power than the target audience. If you are in a leadership role, imagine yourself as a servant to your employees instead of seeing them as your servants. If you work in talent acquisition, think of yourself as the guide that leads your ideal job seekers on the right path to improve their careers and lives. Let them be the heroes calling the shots because they probably do. In whatever role you are in relation to your employees, staff, and job seekers, adopt a frame of mind where you become the guide instead of the hero.

When you approach your target audience thinking you have less power than them, you are more capable of seeing their perspective, which, in turn, helps you detect how to move these people to the goals you have for them. No one is taking away your experience and miles. Instead, those can be better applied when we position ourselves as the guide and let our target audience be the hero. Your company has the combined experience, skills, knowledge, and authority of your people. When your "organization person" uses it all in the role of a guide, you have that much to offer to your target audiences to help them become the heroes they desire.

In employer branding—talent acquisition and leadership, too—we will be way more persuasive when our communication and messages intentionally decrease our power as the employer and increase the power of the talent we want to influence. Those who hold the real power do not always have to prove it. If you like designer clothes, think of this as losing the need to show off labels—those who need to know that you have designer clothes and items will recognize your status without you having to show them off.

But I also want to share this direct quote from Daniel H. Pink, whose work I admire so much: "Don't get the wrong idea, though. The capacity to move others does not call for becoming a pushover or exhibiting saintly levels of selflessness." I believe this reflects the second principle of using your head as much as your heart.

The third component in perspective-taking is the act of strategic mimicking. Humans have natural skills in copying and mimicking the behavior of others, especially when they want to be accepted by specific people and groups. Our need to belong is so strong that we almost automatically mimic behaviors, expressions, accents, and speaking patterns.

I'm like a parrot as I quickly pick up accents. It is so easy that I find it impossible to switch off after a while! When I was seventeen and spent an entire year in the United States as an exchange student, I came home with a strong Midwest accent. But what was funny was that on the long flight home from the US to Finland, I sat beside a girl from the eastern part of Finland with a super strong accent. When my parents met me at the airport, I greeted them with this strong Eastern Finnish accent, and they were like, who is this person? The only Finnish I'd heard for a year was of that girl, and it just stuck to me like glue. To scientists, mimicking is the social glue, and a sign of trust humans show each other when we naturally mirror other people's behavior.

In the context of conversations and comments on social media, as an example, subtle mimicking can look like agreeable comments on posts. Even if you didn't agree with someone doesn't mean you have to attack their opinion vocally or in writing. Especially on social media, we see a lot of disagreeable behavior in comments where total strangers seem to pick a fight on purpose or because they misunderstand your point.

The strategic mimicry that Daniel H. Pink discusses is about intentionally mirroring someone's gestures, tone, or pace of speech—but *subtly*, so it fosters rapport without feeling like an imitation. Imagine you're in a meeting with someone you don't know beforehand. They speak in a relaxed, soft tone and occasionally lean back in their chair when making a point. To use strategic mimicry, you'd respond in a similarly

STORY-DRIVEN EMPLOYER BRANDING

calm tone and a more open and relaxed body language without copying directly. This subtly aligns your behavior with theirs, which can make them feel more comfortable and trust you, as people tend to warm to those who reflect their own style. The key here is subtlety. If the other person feels that you're mimicking every gesture or word choice, it may come off as mocking or manipulative. When done correctly, mimicking creates a sense of ease and familiarity—two elements that naturally build trust.

## *The Six Principles of Persuasion*

Psychologist Robert B. Cialdini, a professor emeritus at Arizona State University, is a pioneer in the psychology of persuasion. He has developed six principles of persuasion that have become well used in business schools and boardrooms.

What got me interested in the science of persuasion back in the day was this question asked by Cialdini: "If you knew simple changes in the ways you communicate that get people to say yes, wouldn't you want to learn?" "Heck, yes," I said to myself.

So, let's talk next about how you can become elegantly persuasive in your employer brand communication and marketing, applying Cialdini's six principles of persuasion in your employer brand messages, communication, and marketing. If it helps you, think about these as strategies to convince your talent audience to:

- Believe in what you say (as the messenger).
- Favor what you do (as an employer).

- Want to act on what you ask because it is beneficial for *both* them and your organization.

I want to emphasize the importance of benefits for both parties because there is a fine line. Marketing messages that express benefits only for your company can easily sound manipulative. Always look for a win-win to maintain good ethics in your communication and marketing.

## #1 Reciprocity

Reciprocity is probably one of the most powerful tactics for persuading others because humans tend to have good hearts and don't want to feel like they are in debt to someone. When you, as the employer, give first, most people feel obligated to return the favor.

Let's do a test. Think about someone who complimented you on something totally out of the blue. You felt wonderful, but also grateful for the person for their kind gesture that made you feel special. When you think about that moment and that person, don't you feel warmth toward them and almost an obligation to give back?

This first principle taps into behavioral psychology. Our gratefulness makes us want to reciprocate and give something in return so that we do not appear greedy, unappreciative, or, worst of all, totally self-centered! Reciprocity works only when you, as the first giver, choose a favor that isn't significant enough to feel like you deserve something back but significant enough for the recipient to feel like you did go above and beyond.

During Phase One: Winning Sustainable Attention, apply reciprocity in the form of helpful comments, sharing value-added news, insight and information, or connecting people in your target audience with each other or your other contacts when you feel they can help each other. These posts, comments, reshares, tagging people, and mentions must aim to help others.

You want to use your employer brand profile to lend your expertise, connections, and look for ways to help your audience first. The more personalized you can make this, the stronger your impact will be. Remember that reciprocity only works if you initiate the "process" by acting first. You must be genuine because people can pick up if you have ulterior motivations rather than just lending a hand and being kind.

These acts of reciprocity in employer branding help you to win sustainable attention, which lead to growing your organic audience on social media. The benefit of social media is that it doesn't matter if your followers are your ideal future employees or not. What matters is that you can win their attention and grow their awareness about your organization as a place to work in ways that help them decide whether they want to continue to follow, recommend, or advocate you to their networks or end up unfollowing you.

This practice qualifies them as your early-stage audience, and they will continue to follow and engage with your company if your organization resonates with them through your content. If people do not follow back, your profile and content must be re-evaluated. Is the profile you use in employer branding targeted to specified talents, or is it really targeted to anyone specifically, leading to no one being able to relate with your profile and content?

Are your employer brand messages clear and authentic? Is your content providing them with added value, or is it only about you? Most of your employer brand content must be created with the idea that whoever sees your content doesn't know you yet. And all your content must resonate with them so that they can start the Talent Journey and begin forming favorable feelings about your organization person.

## #2 Scarcity

The funny thing with humans is that we always want what we can't have or what soon becomes unavailable. I'm sure you can recognize when you made a purchase because the price was promoted as a discounted price, becoming unavailable shortly. At least, I fall into this trap too often, even though I know why they do this! This principle is based on a psychological phenomenon when people assign more value to less available opportunities. We are so attracted to limited editions and availability or feeling like a VIP (very important person). This key principle is heavily used in TV shops, where you see the timer ticking backward, reminding you constantly this "fantastic opportunity" will soon be out of your reach. Humans are simply more motivated to act when they are set to lose something. Our minds work in mysterious ways!

In employer branding, we can't play with prices, but we can take the advantage of expiring opportunities and exclusive offers. I know this book is not about recruitment marketing, but I want to emphasize, because of how our minds work, never post or promote a career opportunity without an expiration date. The fear of missing out, also known as FOMO, makes us act.

Let's talk about how you can take advantage of "scarcity" in employer branding to win sustainable attention. Robert B. Cialdini says that scarcity works only when you point out what is unique about your proposition but then highlight what they stand to lose if they fail to act on it. What this means is that telling people what they gain is less effective than telling them what they stand to lose. In the science of storytelling, this same principle is used when the guide doesn't only cast the desirable vision but also the negative, emphasizing what the hero is set to lose if they choose not to follow the guide's plan. If you only cast a breathtakingly attractive vision, the hero is not compelled to act. Casting only the positive benefits is psychologically less effective than when also casting the losses. You must articulate the benefits and the value of your offer, making it clear what your target audience will miss out on if they choose not to take the action you propose to them in your employer branding message.

Let's say this was simply a proposal to start following your employer branding account on Instagram. You'd want your invitation message to include what type of value they receive from you as your follower but also explain what value they will miss out on if they choose not to follow. Most employers building their employer brands have not considered why anyone outside (or even inside) their organization would want to follow them. It is important to express this on the bios of the social media profiles you regularly use for employer branding because it makes it easier for people to consider what they gain in exchange for giving you their attention. We are living in what I call the information era, where attention is no longer a default but a currency.

Another example is when we ask our staff to act as social media ambassadors for our organization and business. Usually, we ask for participation without offering any value for those employees—even though we expect them to put in extra work. What if you applied this scarcity principle and turned your talent ambassador activities into a limited-availability program with added benefits for the participants who commit to the program? You can use your imagination, resources, and budget to decide the benefits if you give them compelling reasons to increase their desire to participate and commit. Or have people apply for this program, not making it available for everyone because when something is hard to get, we assume it must be good. This kind of barrier of entry increases the perceived value and makes the offer more appealing.

If you organize employer branding events, you can use this principle of persuasion to create VIP or other exclusive offers for a limited number of participants who sign up or show up first, or who stay until the end of the event. Or you can invite a limited number of target talents to join your group at an event of status to your target audience.

The principle of scarcity can be applied throughout the Talent Journey, but it makes a very good tactic—when ethically used—to win sustainable attention. Humans simply don't want to miss out on compelling opportunities that aren't available to everyone.

## #3 Authority

Don't you prefer to follow people of authority and influence and take an expert's word instead of someone unknown? Authority gives people a reason to follow your employer branding account, talent ambassadors, thought leaders, and people managers when they relate to your employer branding messages and organization persona. When someone appears as an authority figure, we automatically place more respect and trust in their words. Organizations empowered by lots of knowledge and expertise in their field are in a prime position to apply the principle of authority.

Cialdini also says that people are more likely to comply with a request from a source of authority, which your experts are also. Think outside the box and consider external industry influencers and spokespeople who could add authority to your employer brand through collaborative content and posts. Mind you, they are likely to be entrepreneurs because you probably don't want to collaborate with competitors' employees. And in that case, you cannot expect their collaboration to be free of charge. But it can be well worth the investment.

This can be done in multiple ways from Phase One onward as you persuade your relevant talents to join and move forward on their Talent Journeys with your organization.

### 1. Creating thought leadership content for employer branding purposes

Focus on sharing knowledge and expertise that isn't available through multiple other sources; otherwise, your content isn't providing value beyond what many others already provide, and your thought leaders won't be seen as figures of authority. Also make sure the angles chosen for your content are relevant for the peer talents of your thought leaders, not for customers or other business stakeholders.

## 2. Becoming known as "a trusted source of shortcuts" to relevant information

What type of information does your target audience search regularly to help them gain information, inspiration, and examples for their tasks and work-related problems and questions they need solving and answering? If you don't know, organize an ideation workshop with each of your talent segments and have them spend an hour or two producing you these topics.

Humans prefer to receive information in bite-size amounts. Bite-size creates a shortcut our brains are wired to prefer. What if your employer branding content turns your company into a trusted source of shortcuts who your target audience can turn to when they need proven-value content, information, insight, trend reports, and news on the topic of your company's expertise? You don't need to create all these yourself, as part of your employer brand's content plan could include repurposed content from relevant industry sources, news media, and external topic experts.

When people in your target audience repeatedly get such information from you, your company turns into a source of shortcuts, and this helps you win sustainable attention because they will learn to proactively return to your profiles and website. Additionally, this practice helps create distinct employer brand perceptions, allowing you to become known as a specific type of employer who knows a lot about the topics you regularly provide them shortcuts for.

## 3. Becoming an authority figure for soft values, connecting your company with your relevant target audience on a deeper level

Another magnificent way to win sustainable attention and increase your level of authority as an employer is to become an influencer on a specific topic that connects your "organization person" with your target audience through your company values, beliefs, purpose, and mission.

How you can do this is to create, curate, repurpose, and reshare content that represents your organizational values, beliefs, promises, ways of work, and your culture. These can be quotes, citations of famous people, favorable news articles, studies, and insight on a topic matching your company values and beliefs. This way, people in your target audience are able to connect with your company on a deeper, more emotionally driven level when your posts resonate with them.

Let's summarize how you can make authority work for you in employer branding.

- Use your company experts and thought leaders in your employer branding content targeted at your relevant talent audience. They don't need to create the content, as your employer branding contributors can simply interview them and create the content on their behalf.

- Consider collaborating with external experts who are seen as thought leaders in the eyes of your talent audience, to position yourself in the same trusted "group" as these thought leaders and influencers.

- Become a go-to source and the broadcaster of credible industry insight, trend reports, news, and information relevant to your target talents and presented from the perspective of employment, creating a better life, career development, and developing skills and aptitudes supporting the work they do right now. It is vital to tune the angle to fit employer branding purposes and match the interests of your target talent audiences.

- Help your target audience to connect with your company through softer and more emotionally driven topics bringing out your values, beliefs, morals, ethics, mission, purpose, and promises.

Other subtle cues that emphasize your company's position as an authority and help win sustainable attention are:

- Trappings connected to a certain level of success or power, creativity, and innovation, such as how your office looks, where it is located, or items showcasing the perceptions you want to be attached to your employer brand, such as material, social, or intellectual rewards and possessions.

- Using authentic visuals of how your people dress, from creative dressing to power dressing, when you want to emphasize authority in specific talent segments.

- Using credentials, titles, and achievement statements if your company culture is meritocratic.

## #4 Consistency

People strive to be consistent in their beliefs and behaviors and are attracted to structure, systems, and order. This is the impact of the human brain because consistency, routines, and systems help our bodies conserve energy.

I emphasize consistency all the time in my work, as it is that important in winning sustainable attention but also moving your target talents forward on their Talent Journeys with your company.

Consistency applies to the synchrony of the messages we deliver, the way we behave and what we message. There must also be consistency in reminding our audiences of our existence, showing up on socials regularly. What you do and what you say must be consistent for people to believe in you.

One of the biggest things that bothers me about organizations and businesses is that what they state on their websites, social media, and in the celebratory speeches by their leaders is not a reference to real employee, candidate, and subcontractor experiences. What they say or claim and what their audience experiences creates a sense of distrust and uncertainty for employees and external target audiences. How can they trust their employer if they are inconsistent in their actions and words?

Consistency also applies to the way we treat and speak to our employees and applicants. If one person is held accountable for their actions, everyone should be held accountable. Rules should be applied to all employees equally if there are rules in place.

Inconsistencies in how people are treated can lead to demotivation and resentment and ultimately affect employee retention. Therefore, we should be utterly mindful that what we state as our employee value propositions and in our employer branding messages match the actual experiences of our employees and job candidates.

A big part of consistency in our actions is holding people accountable and creating psychological pressure to keep and deliver on our promises. When our audience experiences consistency, they trust us more.

Consistency can be applied in multiple ways in employer branding and achieving sustainable attention from your internal and external audiences:

**#1 Commit to consistent communication and demonstration of your employer brand Key Story Themes.**

Your Key Story Themes are connected to your desired employer brand perceptions. The more you stick to creating content, communicating, and advocating your Key Story Themes in your visual, verbal, and written employer brand content and throughout your employer brand activities, the faster you will achieve your desired employer brand perceptions.

The more you let in content and messages outside your Key Story Themes, the more the consistency gets broken, and your audience gets confused about who you are and what you represent. Even though you know who you are and may feel it doesn't change your perceptions, your external audience only knows what you tell them and what they experience in encounters with your company and people. Be mindful of the perceptions your ad hoc ideas and out-of-scope content create.

Show up regularly on social media through content, comments, and posts reflecting your desired employer brand perceptions, as it is the most cost-efficient way to stay consistent in employer branding. You can schedule and automate posts if you find it hard to be regularly present.

**#2 Say no to all random and ad hoc ideas and messages that are not in line with your Key Story Themes.**

You must lead and manage your employer brand perceptions if you are the owner of your organization's employer brand. Half of this responsibility is to say respectfully no to all random and ad hoc ideas, wishes, and even already existing content if it is not in line with your Key Story Themes.

Confusing your target audience results in lost sustainable attention and even in misinterpreted employer brand perceptions that will hurt your talent acquisition.

As you stick to your Master Plan, help your collaborators to understand how they can tune their ideas and existing content to match with one or more of the Key Story Themes. Appreciate people who are willing to contribute but help them take their content and ideas in the direction pertinent to your employer brand goals and objectives.

**#3 Support talent acquisition with timely recruitment communication with all your applicants.**

Both the public recruitment and the personal candidate communication provide your organization a massive opportunity to build a favorable employer brand—or fail in your employer branding efforts—especially if your organization hires a lot and regularly.

Each applicant holds either a positive or a negative perception about you as a potential employer from the moment they start their research on you to when they send their applications until they find out whether they succeeded in your recruitment process or not.

Timely communication is one of the most powerful sources of positive candidate experiences. However, timely does not mean timely based on your schedule, but timely based on their individual expectations.

Let's look at some examples on exercising consistency in your talent acquisition related communication.

- Apply consistent internal communication routines and communicate to your applicants and candidates how they will be kept up to date with the recruitment process. This creates trust in your talent acquisition people and you as an employer.
- Keep up with a regular communication cycle, even when there is nothing new to report.

- Inform about the end of the process for all your applicants and candidates *immediately* when you have decided their time in your process ends here. The worst decision is to mass inform when the entire process is over for you. Be polite and appreciate other people's time and effort. After all, your company was lucky they chose to be available for you instead of your competition.

Remember that showing up consistently is a sign that you care that your organization cares about people. Nothing speaks more volumes of lack of importance than failing to show up. Is that something you want your organization to become known for? I don't think so—not on your watch!

The great thing about committing to consistency is the pressure it creates in others to reciprocate your consistency. No one wants to be the only one who wasn't on time or didn't deliver on promises. Use this to your advantage as you build your Magnetic Employer Brand.

### #5 Likability

Have you noticed how you are easily influenced by similar, complementary, and cooperative people? When someone shows you, they like you, you start to pay attention to them and find yourself liking them back.

The incredible impact of the principle of likability is that it's so hard to say no to a friend! Great salespeople invest in building great relationships with their customers because people tend to do business with their friends—people they trust, like, and enjoy being around.

How do you get people to like you that much in employer branding? You show that you like them first. The more you show you like the people in your target audience, the more you grow their pressure to reciprocate your liking.

Imagine a total stranger starting to follow you on social media and liking tons of your posts at one go. Their expression of liking you immediately triggers your attention and makes you curious to check out their profile (algorithm alert!) and follow you back if your profile seems to match with what they like to see and follow on that specific social media.

Applying this principle of persuasion—likability—on social media can be a huge advantage for you. However, it only works if your profile focuses on building your employer brand and your content is relevant to the people you desire to follow back. Think about your employer brand profile being the profile for your "organization person," whose personality is your culture; values are your company values; morals, ethics, and beliefs represent those of your company; and behavior is akin to how your people behave at work.

From your bio to every single piece of content easily available for a visitor, everything must act as a call to "follow me" for people relevant to your business and matching with your target audience. If you can do this on your employer brand profiles on social media, likability will be a fun tactic for you to regularly repeat, because it will attract your ideal and relevant target audience members to follow and connect with your employer brand "persona."

## #6 Consensus–also known as social proof

The sixth and last key principle by Professor Robert B. Cialdini is consensus, also known as social proof.

People tend to make choices that seem popular among others. We feel the risk is lower when proven by others we can relate to. This is why customer and employee testimonials are used in marketing. However, even more persuasive social proof comes from genuine mentions of your organization by people in your target audience who have become your raving fans through your employer branding content and actions as you apply the science of persuasion.

All we need is to create a social media profile dedicated to employer branding, with the idea that this profile is the profile of our "organization person." Then, we commit to consistently applying The Magnetic Employer Branding Method™ and the science of persuasion to proactively engage with and grow our network. For this, I recommend Instagram or TikTok at the time of writing this book.

Log in to your employer brand profile and regularly grow your network by following new people. You don't need to know whether they match with your talent audience because they will self-select when your content from your bio to your posts is specific enough to either resonate or not. Start from the users who have liked and engaged with your posts. Check out who follows other companies, authorities, and influencers like yours.

Regularly comment and engage with their posts so that they learn to see you as an active follower of theirs. Let them get to know more about your "organization persona" through your positive and compelling comments on their posts matching your company values, beliefs, ethics, morals, purpose, mission, promises, and passions. They will most certainly follow you back if you act human through your employer branding profile.

The bigger your audience grows, the more social proof it creates. However, you must make this a qualitative activity, not quantitative, because you also want most of your followers to be your relevant talent audience.

Social proof works because when people are unsure, they look around for proof of trust and low associated risk with their decision-making about your organization.

Thanks to Professor Robert B. Cialdini's pioneering work, we don't even need to dive too deeply into the actual science part of persuasion if we follow his six principles. However, a fine line exists between being positively persuasive and assertive and becoming aggressive and pushy. As we apply The Magnetic Employer Branding Method™, we only pursue the most ethical and elegant forms of persuasion and never manipulate anyone.

## Wrapping up How to Win Sustainable Attention

Instead of posting occasionally, when you have the time or the inspiration, you need to adopt a consistent posting rhythm to keep the invitation phase switched on. When you have your Key Story Themes in place, and you know what employer brand perceptions your content and comments aim to create and strengthen, there are plenty of tools that help you keep up a regular posting cycle.

Positioning the talent as the hero of your employer branding story makes your messages and content valuable to them. It's about what is relevant to them at the time of posting and how your "organization person" can inform, inspire, educate, or entertain them on that topic that helps win sustainable attention.

Remember, the way your "organization person" becomes seen as a trusted advisor is based on how your profile behaves and communicates through your content, comments, and direct messages on social media, in your internal communication and recruitment, and candidate communication. Trust is built by showing up consistently with value-added information, being a great communicator, keeping your promises, and showing empathy and kindness to your target audience members.

Who doesn't want to follow and pay attention to an inspiring, caring, and empathic guide?

There is no reason in this world why your company could not own such a position in the eyes of your talent target audience. It all boils down to what your content and posts consist of and how your employer brand profile—the organization person—behaves online and offline.

Treat your company as a human, an organization person, who has the entire organization's resources, insight, expertise, and sense of humor available for content creation and value-add comments. You, as the reader and possibly the employer brand owner, do not have to carry all the wisdom if you curate the information, you have access to according to your Key Story Themes and their relevant angles to your target audience.

Try to apply the narrative content format and some persuasive communication principles in your content and posts.

This is the path to winning sustainable attention from your target audience. When you follow these practices regularly, you don't have to start repeatedly pursuing their attention. Instead, they will become ready to move forward with your "organization person" on their Talent Journey.

Now, it is time to get to know each other better and move to Phase Two: Growing Employer Brand Awareness.

## CHAPTER 11

# Phase Two: Growing Employer Awareness

"There are leaders, and there are those who lead. Leaders hold a position of influence. Those who lead inspire us. Whether individuals or organizations, we follow those who lead not because we have to, but because we want to. We follow those who lead not for them, but for ourselves."

SIMON SINEK

## Building Employer Awareness to Become Known for Your Why Instead of Your What

Building your distinct employer awareness is the next phase of the Talent Journey of the Information Era™. Now that you have earned the sustainable attention of your target audience, you need to start connecting their desires, needs, values, and beliefs with the why of your business. The why of your business is the reason your business exists, also known as your company's purpose or mission. If you are unaware of or your employer doesn't have a purpose or a mission, consider asking about this from the top management.

If you don't have access to the top management, reach out to a superior as high up as possible, or head of the marketing or communication department. Alternatively, you can also lean into your company's customer promise or focus on the company values and ways of work (your culture) or your EVPs (employer value propositions).

Building employer awareness comes before employer branding because you want to make sure your target audience forms a distinct and authentic employer image about your company as an employer and a workplace. This phase is often skipped because the company is so well known among their customers. However, how your company has been positioned and perhaps even branded among customers is not based on who you are as an employer but on your products and services. That is not a representation of your authentic "organization person" but of make-believe. You want to make sure your role and position as an employer is based on truth, not on make-believe.

Think of this phase like starting to date someone. You as the "organization person" pursue talents with the purpose of getting to know each other, casually over time, until both parties recognize "that something special" in each other needed to move forward toward becoming either exclusive or best friends. Growing your employer awareness is like courting and dating, while the building employer brand affinity phase (coming up next) is equal to getting serious about each other with the intent of an exclusive relationship.

Let me take you through this dating analogy.

## 1. Winning sustainable attention is like watching someone charming across the room.

When people first pay proper attention to your company in the role of an employer, it's like spotting someone attractive at a party. As your eyes lock on each other, you become curious about the other person, but that's all that happens that evening. Your "organization person" needs to stand out with distinct charm, personality, and approachability if we want our target audience to lock eyes with ours. Your "organization person's" charm and personality are your company's culture, values, and atmosphere oozing through your content and messages.

How does a one-time event become sustained attention? If you never see the person whose eyes are locked with yours, you will forget about them. Someone else replaces them in your mind. The same happens with organizations whose employer branding strategy is occasional campaigns supporting pending recruitment efforts. To win sustainable attention and have a chance to learn more about each other requires your organization person to be regularly present where your target audience hangs out. And that place is online.

**2. Those first impressions matter.**

Just like a promising first date, the initial content or interaction that someone has with your brand must intrigue and engage. Poor communication or lack of effort—just like showing up late or being disinterested—can break the connection before it starts. Commenting on their posts is a way to keep your company on top of their minds. Engaging with those who comment on your employer brand posts is equally important.

**3. Building trust is a two-way street.**

In dating, you take time to understand each other's needs, wants, and aspirations. Similarly, employer branding during the awareness phase should show, not only focus on, what life looks like as part of your organization. Spending some time weekly—even if just fifteen minutes—showing genuine interest in your followers and other target audience members' content gives you access to learn from their posts what's on their mind and show them you are interested in them. Just make it personal, sharing your first name in your comments, as you don't want to appear a faceless organization.

**4. From flirting to serious conversations.**

As awareness grows, it's time to transition from the playful, surface-level attraction to deeper conversations about what it's really like to work in your organization. Share authentic employee stories and behind-the-scenes moments, demonstrate your company's mission, vision, purpose, values, beliefs, ethics, and morals through your content and make your company's level of knowledge and experience known through substance-knowledge content.

**5. It's not about attracting everyone.**

In dating, trying to appeal to everyone usually backfires. The same is true for employer branding. By staying authentic to who you are as an "organization person," your values, aspirations, and beliefs help your internal and external audience members self-select your organization as the right talents become attracted to what your organization represents and find alignment in how you see the future for you and them. These are your unique selling points.

Employer awareness is the extent to which your target audience is familiar with you as an employer and your workplace. They know about you as an employer beyond your company's name and logo, but you haven't become their "chosen one" just yet. Building your employer awareness means consistently ensuring your organization is at the forefront of relevant people's minds when they think about your industry and employers within it.

You must be specific about how becoming part of your why influences your people and paves their way for a better life.

To become an inspirational employer, you must act and communicate from the inside out to grow the awareness of your target audience of why they should care about you as an employer, company, and organization. But don't make it about you; make it about them. Instead of talking about "us, we, and our needs and aspirations" directly, position the talent at the center and make them understand where the alignment can be found. This is the key element in ultimately successful employer brand communication. You don't need to talk so much about you when you simply talk about the topic.

You will learn if someone loves sailing when they post about sailing a lot. They don't need to mention they love sailing. The topic makes it clear. They can post pictures of the sunset taken on a sailing trip. Or share tips about what is easy to cook on the boat, curate the latest news from an ongoing sailing competition, instruct what to pack on a month-long sailing trip, or how to sail safely with a baby on board. These are all connected to sailing but aren't about them as the hero and more of a guide sharing value-added insight with their audience. You would surely become aware that they are experienced in sailing, even if they never mentioned it.

Focus on creating awareness content from your why, inside out. You will help your target audience to recognize who you truly are as an employer and a place to work, just like they would get to know your "organization person." This builds trust and triggers your audience to connect with you on a much deeper level, making it more likely for many of them to become emotionally impacted by what your company represents.

# The Importance of Growing Employer Awareness for Companies Going Through Change

Change is no stranger to most companies and their employees. Since digitalization really kicked off—I mark it with Facebook becoming globally popular in 2007—constant change became the norm for humans and companies. Digitalization refers to the adoption and integration of digital technologies into everyday processes, transforming how businesses and we individuals operate as consumers, employees, and job seekers day-to-day. This magnificent change involved converting information "from paper" into digital formats and leveraging technology to improve efficiency, accessibility, and innovation. Many jobs disappeared as a result, but many new ones were also born from digitalization.

Before digitalization, companies had significant power of knowledge over consumers, employees, and job seekers. Today, almost everyone has access to information, and this has removed a lot of power from companies to consumers, employees, and job seekers. If your company isn't willingly accessible online, and not just on your website but on social media, your company doesn't exist.

Companies continue to go through change for other reasons too, such as changes in the top management or ownership, starting to execute a new strategy, mergers and acquisitions, or other similar fundamental changes that impact employee and leadership experiences day-to-day. It is equally important to grow existing perceptions of your

STORY-DRIVEN EMPLOYER BRANDING

target audiences inside and outside your company to match with the new stage in the life of your company.

The Magnetic Employer Branding Method™ with the Talent Journey communication framework provides you with a solid structure and plan to enforce the internal change just the same. Now you need to convince your existing people of a promising future for them, despite the harder times organizational changes will bring along. Instead of focusing on your external target audience, you are inviting your existing staff to take part in your company's change journey and build their awareness, commitment, and contribution to making the change happen. Otherwise, your company risks retention, decreasing employee satisfaction and lack of commitment to change.

Your change in communication efforts will be so much more successful when you frame your messages to position your staff as the hero and your company as their trusted guide. This means that instead of sharing information and creating content where you focus on what the company in third person will do and must achieve, you frame all the messages to "we, us together, and you."

The communication framework helps you to take your staff on the change journey with you, instead of inviting them to step in only when the company already made it there. Commitment is built during the journey through participation. This employer branding methodology gives them a role in the change process, making it easier to accept it, contribute to it, and welcome it.

# The Benefits of Focusing on Growing Employer Awareness Before Branding

Even though long-lasting love stories have been born from "love at first sight," usually such commitment is based on a strong friendship that grows into companionship and love. The awareness phase represents building that friendship, trust, and loyalty before locking "love" into it. This is an important phase in employer branding because this is where the alignment happens over time, learning and witnessing both good and bad times and understanding whether our values, beliefs, morals, and ethics align, also when they become tested.

The higher your target audience's awareness is about you in your employer role, the more your target audience is likely to trust you to have the same direction and becoming employed by this company is most likely to help them build the future they desire. When the trust *in this* has been built, emotional connection is bound to happen, and that means your target audience positions your company as their number one option. High employer awareness is not just about being known but being known for the right reasons by the right audience and in the right ways (the desired employer perceptions).

Even though employer branding has been attached to activities such as creating recruitment videos and content-strong recruitment campaigns, you need to know that is not employer branding. A brand creates an emotional connection by resonating deeply with its audience's values, aspirations, and challenges. It goes beyond logos and slogans to evoke feelings, whether it's trust, inspiration, or belonging, by understanding and reflecting the audience's identity and desires.

When a brand helps its audience envision themselves in a desired position, it acts as a mirror, showing them the version of themselves they want to present to their stakeholders—be it as confident professionals, visionary leaders, or caring employers. Through storytelling, visuals, and tone, a strong brand fosters this aspirational identity. Branding, at its core, is about making the audience feel good about themselves. It's not about shouting, "Look how great we are!" but rather whispering, "Look how great you are with us." This emotional alignment strengthens loyalty and motivates action, as people are naturally drawn to brands that affirm their values and elevate their sense of self-worth.

When you focus on making sure your target audience has the right perceptions and understanding of your organization inside out, like it was a person, your employer branding efforts will seal their deal with you. The whole employer branding process is a transformation journey where you help your target talents recognize what is truly important for them in their lives and how you can help them fulfill their aspirations for their lives and careers.

When their awareness of you is on solid grounds, and they strongly align with what your company represents to them as an employer, organization, and community of other talents, moving them from the friend zone to the brand zone is a cup of fine English tea.

## Wrapping up How to Grow Employer Awareness Really Well

In the Talent Journey of the Information Era™, employer awareness precedes employer branding. This phase is about establishing a genuine, distinct image of your organization as an employer, rooted in purpose and culture, rather than the jobs you hire for or the benefits and career opportunities you offer.

Drawing parallels to dating, this is like the "getting to know you" stage: earning curiosity, building trust, and fostering meaningful connections with your target audience.

**1. Start with Your Why:** Your "why"—the purpose or mission of your business—should resonate with your audience's values and aspirations. Also include your company values, beliefs, vision for the future, your key leadership principles, and why these are so meaningful that you base the success of your organization on them. This alignment inspires interest and builds trust, making your employer identity more authentic and relatable.

**2. Be Present and Consistent:** Winning attention requires consistent visibility where your audience spends time, especially online. Sporadic campaigns won't suffice; sustained engagement keeps you on their radar. What kind of friend is a person who only shows up when they need something from you? This is about the most important people in your business operations, so make your actions human.

**3. Build Trust Through Engagement:** Employer awareness grows through genuine interactions, such as commenting on posts and showing interest in your audience's world. This reciprocity fosters trust, just like a budding friendship.

**4. Focus on Authenticity:** Employer awareness is about being known for the right reasons. This is where you build your desired employer brand perceptions and remove any outdated or otherwise untrue perceptions. Your values, culture, and employee experiences should shine through your content, helping your audience self-select based on alignment with your ethos. As an employer, the worst-case scenario is that you sold apples for oranges, your current and future employees become gruntled and dissatisfied, and lose their trust in you.

**5. The Role of Awareness in Change:** During organizational changes, growing employer awareness among internal audiences builds trust and commitment. Framing employees as heroes of the change story fosters participation and eases transitions.

Ultimately, employer awareness creates a foundation of trust and emotional connection. By focusing on your "why," understanding your audience, and consistently delivering authentic messages, you inspire alignment. This lays the groundwork for deeper relationships and a strong employer brand. As in great partnerships, it's not about you—it's about how your organization enables your audience to thrive.

## CHAPTER 12

# Phase Three: Building Employer Brand Affinity

*"If Nike owned a hotel, we would probably recognize it. If Hyatt (a hotel chain) made sneakers, we wouldn't be able to identify them because Hyatt doesn't have a brand. They have a logo. Hotels at that price point, the Hyatts, Hiltons, and Mariotts, all look the same. I don't know where I am [when I step into the reception lounge]."*

SETH GODIN

E mployer brand affinity can be defined as your talent audience's feelings and emotional connections toward your company as a place to work. Brand affinity refers to the emotional connection employees and candidates feel toward your employer brand. It's not just about knowing what the brand stands for; it's about genuinely *caring* and feeling aligned with your company's values, mission, morals, ethics, and culture on a personal level.

When people experience employer brand affinity, it impacts them deeply:

**In their hearts:** They feel a sense of pride and belonging. They believe in the company's purpose and see themselves as an integral part of something meaningful. This emotional attachment fuels loyalty and commitment.

**In their minds:** They trust the organization and feel confident in its direction. They see their work as valuable and aligned with their own aspirations, leading to a sense of purpose and clarity.

**In their souls:** They connect with the company on a deeper, almost intrinsic level. It's not just a job; it's a place where they feel seen, valued, and inspired to be their authentic selves, fostering motivation and a sense of fulfillment, building their self-confidence and self-awareness.

This emotional connection strengthens internal culture, enhances employee advocacy, and makes the company a place where people *want* to stay and thrive—not just because they need to, but because they *choose to*. Affinity helps the target person feel elevated, empowered, inspired, important, valued, respected, special. Being associated with your employer *brand* attaches value and status in their character in the eyes of their peers and networks. This then builds their self-confidence, impacts their self-awareness, and makes them feel good about their life and confident about their future prospects. That's what a Magnetic Employer Brand means to me as the mother of this methodology.

Imagine if your organization—how your company does what it does and how your people and management make each other feel—could provide your target audience a vision of an emotionally inspiring future? That the way you communicated your Magnetic Employer Brand would paint an inspiring vision of a better life and better future for your target audience. As the outcome of your regular employer brand communication and content, they felt a strong emotional connection with your organization, understood how people inside your organization are bonded by specific reasons that give them a sense of purpose and align them through their mutual beliefs and values of life. These people outside your organization would become strongly compelled by also being part of the company's story— and not any part but the hero's role with you in the role of the employer providing them with a vision, mission, and guidance in the form of goals and objectives of work and a supportive leadership culture. That's what real employer brand affinity means to me.

Many employers struggle to get their employees to advocate for the company. Imagine if you didn't even have to ask. And, what if employer brand advocacy wasn't even limited to your existing employees? What if your employer brand influenced your external audience in ways that they recommended and advocated for your company willingly because it added to their status in the eyes of their peers? We all are familiar with brand affinity when it comes to consumer products we favor and artists we idolize. You can achieve the same with employer branding. When your internal and external talent audiences have a strong emotional connection with your employer brand, they are deeply moved by what your brand represents for them. The stronger the employer brand affinity, the more vocal your audience becomes about your employer brand.

Creating and growing employer brand affinity must be your primary goal in employer branding. It describes the emotional connection individuals in your talent target audiences have for your company as a place to work. The stronger the connection, the stronger the employer brand affinity. What this means is your company ultimately positions itself as the most preferred employer for talents relevant and ideal for your business. However, promoting the talent acquisition needs of your company, regardless of if you wrapped them in gold and sparkle, doesn't make your target audience love you. That's why I created this methodology applying business storytelling in employer branding.

## The Role of Business Storytelling in Building Your Employer Brand

We all love our people's stories and company success stories. Can you guess why? It's because we were part of creating those stories. That's why they matter to us. Having a role in something significant is meaningful to *us*. However, just because something is interesting and important to you doesn't automatically make it relevant to someone else, especially when they had no part in it. Business storytelling turns the tables around and reframes your organization's stories into stories your target audience can imagine being part of.

I absolutely love the way many organizations invest in recruitment videos and other content, helping them to get more attention to their recruitment campaigns. However, there is a long way from recruitment marketing to building employer brand affinity. While content and digital marketing are fantastic tools for modern marketing, using them in your campaigns won't automatically make talents love you. Not even like you.

Creating and growing employer brand affinity is at the core of building a modern employer brand. Brand affinity aims to tap into the emotions in your relevant target audience because emotions drive our motives and actions. Employer brand affinity is about a mutual belief we share, common values, ideologies, and beliefs. These shared values and beliefs contribute to a relationship, also growing brand loyalty and impacting your talent audience's attitudes, behavior, and decisions when it comes to their careers and lives and your company as part of those. That's the essence of "building the modern employer brand."

But before you can even get there, you need to win sustainable attention and grow employer awareness and a level of loyalty comparable to dating exclusively. While you are not thinking about a marriage just yet, you are loyal to finding out whether this could lead to a permanent contract. In this methodology, your target audience's loyalty refers to something so simple

STORY-DRIVEN EMPLOYER BRANDING

as to when they are on social media and browse through their feeds and see your employer brand content, they make the effort of lifting their fingers and tapping "like" and even commenting or sharing your post to their network. You know how proper love isn't the same as a one-night stand or dating casually. It needs time to grow and mature as you get to know each other, searching for that "click."

Employer brand affinity is a hugely valuable asset for organizations, but it is also very important to us human beings. We are wired to be part of a tribe, and employer brand affinity sets the stage for becoming part of a tribe. A tribe isn't tied only to being an employee in the organization. It happens less in work life, but think about your favorite bands or sports teams. The same act of affinity takes place when you are a raving fan of a team or an artist. In fact, I once helped an e-gaming company with their values, and they are a great example of an employer whose brand isn't limited to their potential employees but also to their fans who share their values and ethics in the field of e-gaming. You don't need to be part of the team—a player in an e-gaming team, a guitarist in your favorite band, or an athlete in your favorite NHL team—to experience being part of the tribe.

A global technology company, Reaktor, hails from Finland. They have always been known for their high-performance, sophisticated, and elite software culture. Back in the day, when the company was smaller and the founders were still managing the company day-to-day, they had a very emotionally impactful employer brand. Even though we were never in a client-relationship, I popped over at their Helsinki headquarters every once in a while, for a cup of coffee and a chat. Every time I visited their office, I left with some merchandise. When you saw others on the Helsinki city streets also wearing their merch, you immediately associated belonging to the same tribe and feeling exclusive. Their culture of exclusive and high-quality actions and their organization's behavior created stories people loved sharing. Those stories pulled people toward wanting to be part of their tribe: as employees or other stakeholders. I felt it too! I was also proud to be part of their tribe in the role I would describe as an advisor to their employer branding and talent acquisition and an entrepreneur-friend to their founders.

Business storytelling isn't limited to others telling favorable stories about us. We can adopt it as our communication strategy and use the science of storytelling to captivate the minds of our target audiences.

Author and scientist Jeff Hawkins published a book called *A Thousand Brains: A New Theory of Intelligence* in 2021. The book is about the neocortex, the largest area of the human brain. The neocortex is the wrinkly area at the top of our skulls, often characterizing the brain. This part of the brain creates our language and allows us to plan, think, hear, and create perceptions. That's why Hawking calls it the organ of intelligence. When we listen to stories, the neocortex becomes activated as it tries to make sense of the narrative.

What makes stories so incredibly impactful is that they trigger multiple simultaneous activities in our brains to work together. Stories are one of a kind, as no other type of information provokes our emotions and makes us feel the excitement, sorrow, anger, empathy, enthusiasm, and even fear.

However, hearing stories isn't limited to only triggering emotions. There is way more to the neuroscience behind a human's dependence on stories. We love stories so much because four vital chemicals are released in our brains when we hear a good story. These chemicals are called dopamine, oxytocin, cortisol, and endorphins. Each of these chemicals has a unique role in how stories impact our brains. It is incredible that there is a scientifically proven communication formula we can all learn to apply, and it triggers such an extraordinary impact on the recipient.

Let's look at these chemicals closer. You probably have heard of them before.

#### #1 Dopamine

Dopamine is the natural "dope" that makes you sensitive to your feelings. I always remember it as the glue sticking the information provided by the story to the audience's memory. We copywriters use "hooks" as the starting sentences of the copy-text. These hooks help induce dopamine in your story. Hooks can be catchy headlines or opening statements that pique the reader's curiosity. For instance, using powerful keywords like "revealed," "unveiled," or "secret" can instantly generate interest in what you have to say.

Hooks spark an emotional reaction and create a sense of urgency for your audience to continue reading, listening, or watching. They excite the audience with a promise and anticipation of something worth their time and attention. I believe a movie trailer has the same purpose. Hooks are essential because whether it's humor, fear, anger, or nostalgia, tapping into these feelings will make your content more memorable and relatable.

## #2 Oxytocin

Oxytocin, also known as the love hormone or trust hormone, is released when we are touched gently by someone, like when we get a hug, a kiss, or lean on someone we care about. Even a handshake in a business meeting can release oxytocin and build trust between you and the other person. Shaking hands means committing to keep your promise. Oxytocin is released during birth, as it is nature's way of helping mothers form an instant bond with the newborn. The release of oxytocin also helps create a connection with the person telling the story, making us feel that we can trust the storyteller. It evokes empathy, which is essential in trust. Vulnerability and honesty are some of the key ways to evoke empathy and cause oxytocin releases in the audience.

As the business storyteller, these make you feel more human, which builds trust and connectivity between you and your audience. When building your employer brand, this hormone is quite an asset. It makes your target audience feel more connected to you and grows trust in you, your messages, and who you represent.

One great technique is to reveal the secret thoughts of the storyteller. These hidden thoughts are equivalent to the discussions happening in our brains. Our impulses, reactive thoughts, anxiety, nerves, or obsessions characterize most thoughts we prefer to keep to ourselves. But they can also be dreams we are too embarrassed to express. We would rather not show these hidden sides to others because we fear they would think less of us or reject us. Many business leaders prefer not to be transparent about their fears, mistakes, or the heartaches of the businesses they lead when transparency like that, even in small doses, can have a hugely positive effect on the attractiveness of the company as a business and a workplace.

Author Lisa Cron calls these "secret thoughts" and information *story juice*. These hidden thoughts are such a vital part of a story that without them, there isn't a story. Examples of secret thoughts are:

- *"I hope he doesn't look at me differently after he sees I have this massive pimple on my cheek."*
- *"That person hurt me so badly, it broke all the trust between us, and I will never forget them."*
- *"I hope my boss sees this great feedback I received from an important client. I bet it would make her appreciate my input more."*

Story juices illuminate the story, giving it the necessary drama and bringing the story to life. They are not the story we see unfolding in front of us. Instead, they are the conversations in the characters' minds, indicating how they make sense of what is happening as they struggle. These hidden thoughts are the transformation that is crucial for the story to move forward.

You only need to think about a movie or a book that bored you before the story started because you felt it was stagnant and not moving forward fast enough to keep you interested. The story is always set on transformation: the internal change the character goes through as the story's plot moves forward.

According to Cron, all stories are character driven. It doesn't matter whether the characters and events are fictional, the human brain processes fictional events and characters as if those were happening to us in real life. I'm sure you, too, have heard plenty of stories where what happened to the main character (the hero) made you feel empathetic toward them and want to know what happens next. Those inner thoughts, the story juices, kept you glued on the story. This same formula applied in our employer brand content will have the same impact on our target audience.

## #3 Cortisol

Cortisol is known as the stress hormone. It is our natural alarm that controls our mood, motivation, and fear, and it helps us focus. Our cortisol levels shoot up when we are in danger or under constant stress and anxiety. Similarly, events in a story may trigger the stress hormone, commanding our brain's attention. When our cortisol levels are high, we are alarmed, pay attention, and are ready to learn a lesson. When we don't want to lose our audience's attention, our story needs to sustain attention and offer some intense moments that release cortisol to trigger attention.

## #4 Endorphins

Endorphins are chemicals that make us feel oh-so-good. They make us feel happy and connected and put us at ease. Stories also release endorphins, making the audience more receptive to your information. No other type of

STORY-DRIVEN EMPLOYER BRANDING

communication or format of information impacts the human brain like a story, making all this happen simultaneously as we listen to, hear, or watch stories. Stories are stories only when all these activities occur in the brain. As a result, your messenger and the message become remembered, trusted, enjoyed, emotionally connected to, and loved. When your employer brand stories trigger these chemicals in the brains of your employees and external target audiences, they make those people feel good, and oh boy, do they come back for more! Can you imagine how effective employer branding can be when we use storytelling in our messaging and content?

## Evoking Emotions is Key in Favorable Decision-making

Christine Comaford is a neuroscience expert and *New York Times* bestseller who says our emotions power 90 percent of our behavior and decision-making. We may want to believe we are rational and logical decision-makers, but we make decisions on emotional grounds and look for some rationale to back them up. If you want your audience to believe in your word, agree with you, and take action that is favorable to you, you want to veto their emotions instead of their logic. It makes scientific sense to use stories in your communication as a leader, employer, HR, recruiter, or anyone using communications and marketing to get people to believe in your words and follow your lead.

Earlier, I mentioned neuroscientist Dr. Paul J. Zak. His research has shown that character-driven stories provoking emotion help the audience better understand and memorize our key messages. He has stated that stories blow the standard PowerPoint presentations to bits when it comes to making an impact. And that is precisely what you want from employer branding.

In her book *Stories for Work*, author Gabrielle Dolan pinpoints the impact of stories based on an investigation into autobiographical memories as follows:

- Emotionally charged events are remembered better.

- Pleasant memories are remembered better than unpleasant memories.

- Positive memories contain more contextual details, which helps memorize details.

- Strong emotion can impair memory for less emotional events experienced at the same time.

- Emotional arousal helps memorize information better, not the importance of information.

She further states, "Too many business leaders believe that sharing an important message, such as a new strategy, is reason enough for their audience to listen." The importance of the message is always subjective. What is important to you may not be necessary to me, and I'm to decide, unless you appeal to my emotions and make me relate to the information so that I understand why I should pay attention.

Business storytelling uses the exact same storytelling structure and impacts the brain exactly the same way as any other authentic story. We just apply the story formula in the context of business and work life to get across important messages and desired perceptions in our internal and external target audiences and stakeholders.

## A Story Structure

A **story structure** is like a road map for telling a tale. It helps you guide the audience from the beginning to the end in a way that makes sense and keeps them interested. Think of it as having three main parts:

**The Beginning (Setup):** This is where you set the stage. Introduce the main character (in employer branding, this might be an employee or team) and their situation. What's their role? What are they facing? You're answering, "Who are we talking about, and what's going on?"

Example: "Anna joined our company as a junior developer, fresh out of university and eager to prove herself."

**The Middle (Conflict or Challenge):** Here's where the excitement happens, and this is the most important part of the story. Here, the character faces a challenge, problem, or obstacle. This is what keeps people interested—we all love a bit of drama or tension! In employer branding, the challenge could be a tough project, career growth struggle, or adapting to change. What is vital is that this challenge gets an unreasonable amount of attention.

Storytelling writers like to describe it as agitating the problem. This part is usually the part that employers feel timid about and prefer to take it out, even though it is crucial for the wanted impact. Without this part, the target audiences are unable to emotionally connect with the situation and end up losing their interest in the whole content.

Example:

"When Anna was asked to lead a critical project, she felt nervous and unsure because of [and this is where you go into details]. [Those events and experiences described here] had made her feel [descriptions of doubt, lack of self-confidence, unhappiness, etc.], and she felt [crippled by the same emotions again]."

**The End (Resolution):** Wrap things up! Show how the character overcame the challenge, what they learned or achieved, and how life looks for them now. This part leaves the audience feeling inspired or satisfied. In employer branding, this is where you emphasize how your company played a role in the resolution, emphasizing your vital part as the guide who enabled the hero to get the remarkable outcome.

Example: "With the support of her team and a mentor [explaining in detail how exactly Anna was convinced and supported], Anna not only delivered a successful project but also got promoted to a senior role within a year. As a result, today Anna is [...] and feels [...] and this experience helped her [...] again."

**In short:** A story structure is the order in which the plot of events is narrated to the audience from a beginning (introduce the person) to the middle (what challenge or opportunity they faced), finishing with an aspirational ending (how they succeeded and grew) relatable to the target audience. It's simple but powerful!

Probably the most well-known story structure is The Hero's Journey by Joseph Campbell. Luke Skywalker's role in Star Wars has been heavily influenced by Campbell's *The Hero with a Thousand Faces.*

The Hero's Journey is about a hero who goes on a quest or an adventure to achieve a goal but is met by multiple obstacles and shaken by fears and doubts before returning home transformed. My storytelling guide, Donald Miller, the author of Wall Street Journal's Bestselling book *Building a StoryBrand*, has simplified the twelve-step The Hero's Journey into a seven-step StoryBrand Formula (SB7) tailoring it to be more applicable to business marketing and storytelling.

*Go to 'What's next? Free Resources That Come with This Book' to download a PDF visualizing the employer brand story formula based on Donald Miller's Story Brand SB7 Formula.*

You can apply this formula in your career stories (we apply this in the Hero Career Story™ template when we write career stories for our clients), social media posts, articles about your company's culture, values, mission and vision, even the business strategy, making it more relatable for your target audience.

We also apply this when we write job posts for our clients and have named our job post template The Magnetic Job Post™. It goes to say, you can apply this story formula in all your employer brand messages, communication, and content, but also your recruitment marketing collateral when you really want to captivate your target audience and compel them to take an action.

In the next section, I explain what other persuasive and emotionally charged methods are applied when building your employer brand based on The Magnetic Employer Branding Method™.

## Summarizing How You Can Build Your Employer Brand Affinity According to The Magnetic Employer Branding Method™

Let's summarize how you can create and grow the magical employer brand affinity. As this is the final phase on the Talent Journey where you provide value for your target audience, we are no longer aiming to grow the awareness or expand the size of our organic audience. Because of your systematic success in winning sustainable attention and growing employer awareness, the most relevant part of your audience is so excited about you that they are now open and eager to connect with your organization on a more personal level.

You don't need to know who they are, as they will let you know. You will start noticing the same people engaging with and commenting on your affinity posts and content in ways that you know they are emotionally affected by those stories and experiences. This allows you to connect and follow them online and engage more regularly with them in a more personal manner, if possible.

During the affinity phase, we aim to build that emotional connection with this part of our target audience to help them identify themselves as part of our story, and for this, we use business storytelling. Your specific objectives at this phase are likely to be connected to engaging your existing employees as your ambassadors or gaining their commitment to your new strategy, culture, or other significant business transformation or change impacting their day-to-day lives as part of your organization. With your external target audience, your objectives are likely to be connected to generating recruitment leads to your recruitment funnel or qualifying ideal and relevant, but currently passive, job seekers as your VIPs to continue to build deeper connections with them until they are ready to discuss career opportunities with you.

The key messages in your employer branding content change their tone from aligning people with their values, beliefs, desires, and needs to be aimed at, during Phases One and Two, to content that provides your target audience social proof such as employee testimonials and transformational stories of your people. These invite the more ideal and relevant target audience members to what I call "self-select" as talents who are most likely to form a strong emotional connection with your brand, purpose, and offer for a better life.

The story structure gives you the perfect formula to outline your key messages into narratives and turn them into more impactful story content. However, you must remember here not to write stories about your company, even if you targeted them internally. Always make your target audience the hero of your story, and make sure you as the employer are their trusted guide. Failure to follow the right roles will turn your target audience on their heels because when people get ready to act, they are looking for inspiration and guidance from an empathetic authority who can help them solve the challenges or get out of the conflict they are struggling with.

## People in Your Target Audience Enter and Move Forward on Their Talent Journeys at Their Own Pace

Inviting part of your talent audience to move forward on the affinity phase does not mean you should stop sharing and publishing content for the previous phases. People start, stop, and move forward on their respective Talent Journeys with your organization at their own time and pace. You don't know who they are and where they are on this journey until they are ready for Phase Three: Building Employer Brand Affinity, as things start to get more personal here. And, you don't need to know. All you need to care about and commit to is keeping this journey "wheel" in motion so that you are actively winning sustainable attention to invite people on their journeys with you and growing employer awareness so that they can recognize mutual interests, views, morals, ethics, and visions for their lives. They will self-select and opt in to stay on a journey with you as long as you give them reasons to do so.

The easiest and most cost-effective means is to do this through regular communication on social media through your content, posts, and comment-conversations. When you commit to pouring out reasons to get to know your "organization person" better, kind of like dating you, the more opportunities they have to move forward or opt out.

And this is what you want, as in the long run, this will increase the quality of your talent acquisition and recruitment and decrease the likelihood of expensive recruitment errors.

So, continue to create content and conversations around your Key Story Themes, but change the angle to individual experiences bringing in feelings, fears, struggles, and how your organization has supported these individuals to overcome those and get to the happy place where they are today. Individuals can be employees, line managers, people in the top management or owners, trainees, summer employees, even job seekers if they are willing to make their experience public. The aim here is to help your affinity audience connect with you through relatable painful experiences and then understand what their future could look like if they took you as their guide and followed your plan to overcome those challenges.

**Examples of this content are:**

- Personal stories where your organization or a specific leader stepped in as a guide to this employee to help them through a difficult time in their life.

- Personally important achievements made possible because of their employment in your organization or because of your values or special benefits or opportunities provided by your company.

- Personal career growth stories where an employee was at a crossroads in their life or career, and becoming employed by your company turned their life around for something better. The story describes where they were, what happened, how your company supported or made the transformation possible, and the happy scenario today.

- Employees' personal experiences as your company went through a change and how someone or something specific in your organization helped them to accept the change and how it wasn't that bad after all. In fact, quite the contrary!

If you have more available resources, such as employee-mentors and team managers, invite their help on this phase. As part of your target audience enters the affinity phase, they want to take a more personal approach with your company. You will notice the same people commenting on your posts regularly, starting to follow some of your people and decision-makers, mentioning your company on socials regularly and sharing your posts to their followers.

They do this because they want you to recognize them and how they idolize your employer brand and what you do. These are examples of them becoming your raving fans. It will be very easy for you to respond by showing them your personalized special attention, rewarding them for the advocacy work they do and inviting them to connect with your organization on a more personal level. Extra pairs of hands and attention are very useful here.

**Examples of how you can provide your affinity-ready audience a more personal experience, a "VIP vibe":**

- Invitation-only events
- Exclusive content for subscribers only
- Personalized gifts
- Automated birthday wishes

Remember, this segment of your overall audience is much smaller than your audience in the awareness phase, so it doesn't have to be a huge and expensive effort for your organization. At my agency, we've invited people at this phase to after-work events at our office with our team to play board games or listen to a keynote speaker on a more personal topic.

What you need to be cautious of is not to turn this phase into make-believe content, slogans and expressions that are not based on your employees' authentic experiences about who you are as an employer, who your "organization person" truly is. A true employer brand is always an authentic representation of the real experiences people will have about your organizational culture, values, morals, and ethics, and you want your "organization person" to express these through its behavior.

When you have access to your target audience like this, you have generated recruitment leads without having to have a vacancy to offer. It's one striking example of how this methodology helps you to convert measurable employer brand value (return on the employer brand investment) as discussed in Chapter 5 from passive job seekers. While it is not the only example of employer brand ROI this methodology can create for your company, it is probably one of the most applied goals and KPIs by the modern employer brand practitioners.

## CHAPTER 13

# Phase Four: Converting Consistent Employer Brand Value

*"If you can't measure it,
you can't improve it."*

PETER DRUCKER

The journey of building a Magnetic Employer Brand doesn't stop at designing a strategy or executing content and communication plans. This chapter focuses on securing and sustaining the return on investment (ROI) of your employer branding efforts, ensuring they continuously serve your organization's strategic goals. By anchoring this process in the Talent Journey of the Information Era™, you unlock long-term value—beyond just recruitment metrics—that can fuel your organization's talent magnetism and business growth for years to come.

## Why ROI Matters in Employer Branding

For many organizations, employer branding is mistakenly seen as a short-term campaign—something to generate applications when the talent pipeline dries up. But with The Magnetic Employer Branding Method™, we aim higher. This isn't about a flash-in-the-pan campaign. It's about creating lasting value that supports talent acquisition, retention, and even broader business outcomes like competitive advantage, employee engagement and joy of work, customer satisfaction and commitment, sales, and as mentioned before, even successful business transformation.

To achieve this, you must shift your mindset: Think of employer branding as an investment, not a cost. Investments require clarity of purpose, intentional strategy, and disciplined evaluation. Without a clear understanding of the ROI, it's easy to lose executive support or underutilize the immense potential of your efforts.

## The Role of the Talent Journey of the Information Era™

The Talent Journey of the Information Era™, the cornerstone of this methodology, ensures that every piece of communication and content plays a role in sequentially building value:

1. **Winning sustainable attention (Phase One)** by breaking through the noise and piquing talent interest.

2. **Growing employer awareness (Phase Two)** to position your brand top-of-mind as a desirable place to work.

3. **Building employer brand affinity (Phase Three)** by creating an emotional connection that resonates deeply with your most relevant and ideal target talent audiences.

The final phase—converting consistent employer brand value—ensures the systematic work done in these phases delivers tangible, measurable returns. Without this phase, the resources poured into earlier stages risk being seen as costs, not investments.

## Clarity, Consistency, and Commitment

This final phase serves as both a reminder and a call to action: You cannot measure what you do not track. To sustain the momentum of your employer branding efforts, clarity around your goals, objectives, and KPIs is non-negotiable.

Here's why:

- **Strategic Goals:** Revisit the goals outlined in your Master Plan. Are you aligning with these consistently, or has execution drifted?

  • **Objectives:** Ensure the smaller, measurable steps you're taking feed into your larger goals. For example, if a goal is to become the employer of choice in your industry, an objective could be achieving 10 percent more direct hires from your priority talent pool this year.

  • **KPIs:** Regularly analyze performance metrics to ensure you're tracking toward those objectives. Remember, KPIs aren't just about applications— they could include talent engagement on LinkedIn, brand sentiment in surveys, or even internal advocacy metrics. Visit Chapter 5 to freshen your memory on the many examples of the KPIs for the objectives you could select in your Master Plan.

## Performance Analysis: The Key to Sustaining the Journey

Without regular performance analysis, it's impossible to understand whether your efforts are yielding the desired outcomes. Think of it this way: A poorly performing campaign might still get applications, but are they quality candidates? Are they aligned with your organizational needs? Will they be able to commit to your culture and values and deliver your customer promise in the way that builds your competitive advantage?

By keeping a finger on the pulse of your performance metrics, you can:

1. Identify what's working and double down on it.
2. Course-correct underperforming initiatives early.
3. Justify continued investments to stakeholders, showing how your work directly contributes to the organization's bottom line.

## *From A Recruitment Tool to Business Asset*

This phase also highlights an essential truth: Employer branding isn't just about filling positions. It's about creating a business asset that—depending on what your specific employer branding objectives are—can, for example:

- Reduce time and cost per hire by generating qualified recruitment leads and building a pipeline of engaged, aligned talent.

- Strengthen employee retention by ensuring the right people join and stay with your organization because they are empowered by your purpose and vision and feel confident and comfortable delivering your business mission and customer promise according to your culture and ways of work.

- Elevate customer and stakeholder confidence by showcasing your organization's purpose and culture and the commitment of your people to your business goals and promises.

When executed with strategy and clarity, employer branding delivers consistent business value that far surpasses recruitment campaigns' fleeting results.

## Final Thoughts: Keeping the Wheel Rolling

The Talent Journey of the Information Era™ is cyclical, not linear. Sustained success relies on continuously analyzing and optimizing your efforts. When you prove the value of your investments, you secure the resources needed to keep the wheel rolling.

This isn't just about keeping the lights on—it's about creating a virtuous cycle where every phase builds on the last, consistently amplifying your employer brand's impact, as your target audience takes the time they need to become convinced no other employer is likely to be as fitting for them as you are.

This framework reminds you of the crucial stages of transformation a job seeker or your existing employee must go through before they are ready to make the move you suggest to them in the form of a new role, strategy, goals, or plans, with your deadlines. It also pre-qualifies people in your target audience for you as they move along this journey toward the change you eventually want to propose to them. Those people who cannot see their future in your organization will naturally opt out during this journey without negative candidate experiences or ill will toward your company. They simply just understand that your company isn't their optimal place to work, possibly saving

SUSANNA RANTANEN

your company a lot of time and money later during and after a recruitment process.

The more time your target audience gives your company, indulging in your content and engaging with your social media profiles and people online, the more likely those who move forward on this journey will be very relevant and very ideal to your company's future. This consistent and ongoing communication process grooms you for them and them for you. If you can see your employer branding more like a marathon instead of a short sprint of a stand-alone campaign, the more valuable outcomes your organization will gain from employer branding.

By treating employer branding as a long-term business strategy—complete with goals, KPIs, and rigorous performance analysis—you ensure that your work is never seen as a one-off project but as a vital driver of your organization's success. And that, dear reader, is how you convert consistent employer brand value into a competitive advantage no one can ignore.

# THE CONTENT PILLARS AND PLAN

## CHAPTER 14

# Content Pillars

*"Storytelling is the most powerful way to put ideas into the world today."*

ROBERT MCKEE

The concept of content pillars in The Magnetic Employer Branding Method™ adds depth and clarity to the employer branding strategy. These pillars organize your content into distinct types aligned with the different phases of the Talent Journey of the Information Era™ (TJIE) and your Key Story Themes. Together, they ensure that your employer brand messaging resonates at every stage of the journey, targeting the unique needs and interests of your audience at the right time. Let's break this down into a compelling, understandable framework that aligns with your goals.

## What Are Content Pillars?

Think of content pillars as content categories designed to serve a purpose at specific stages of your audience's journey with your employer brand. While your Key Story Themes define what topics you'll talk about (the themes), the content pillars guide how and why you'll approach those themes based on the audience's mindset in each phase of their journey. They create structure, ensure consistency, and provide an infinite well of creative content ideas.

Content pillars are not random types of content—they are a matrix that aligns:

1.  Key Story Themes (what you want to communicate)
2.  Talent Journey of the Information Era™ (TJIE) (where the audience is in their decision-making)

## The Three Content Pillars

### *Pillar One: Aspirational and Inspirational Content*

**Purpose:** Win sustainable attention and begin growing employer awareness by sparking curiosity and evoking emotions that resonate with your audience's aspirations.

**Content Focus:** This content positions your target talent as the hero while your company plays the supporting role, offering guidance, values, and ethos that align with the audience's aspirations.

**Content Style:** Lifestyle-oriented, conversational, and relatable content—not work-heavy. It's about showcasing how your values and culture contribute to a better life.

**Content Ratio:** Takes up 60 to 70 percent of your content.

**Examples of Content Ideas:**

- Personal stories from employees who achieved personal or professional breakthroughs.
- Inspirational quotes that align with your Key Story Themes.
- Industry myth-busting content delivered in a relatable, conversational tone.
- Lighthearted, culturally relevant memes or anecdotes.

- Aspirational employee journeys, e.g., "How I Found My Purpose While Growing My Career Here."

## *Pillar Two: Insightful and Informational Content*

**Purpose:** Drive recruitment lead generation and build credibility by showcasing your company's expertise, strategic emphasis, and unique business opportunities.

**Content Focus:** Educational, analytical, and professional content designed to make your target audience feel, "This is the kind of company I want to be part of."

**Content Style:** More concrete and informative than Pillar One, focused on professional appeal.

**Content Ratio:** Takes up 20 to 30 percent of your content.

**Examples of Content Ideas:**

- Industry trends or thought leadership articles written or ghostwritten by your employees.
- Career paths and growth opportunities provided by your organization.
- Insight into your company's customer impact and strategic objectives.
- Professional advice, "how-to" guides, and e-books relevant to your industry.
- Behind-the-scenes content highlighting company innovation and expertise.

## *Pillar Three: Emotional and Tribal Content*

**Purpose:** Build employer brand affinity by fostering emotional connections and loyalty among your audience.

**Content Focus:** Strengthen internal camaraderie and create a sense of belonging to a purpose-driven tribe.

**Content Style:** Emotional, personal, and exclusive-feeling content that nurtures your audience into raving fans.

**Content Ratio:** Takes up 10 to 20 percent of your content.

**Examples of Content Ideas:**

- Employee testimonials about life-changing moments or deeply fulfilling experiences within the company.
- Exclusive content shared with selected audiences (e.g., recruitment leads or alumni).
- Emotional storytelling about challenges overcome by teams and individuals.
- VIP invitations to webinars, workshops, or exclusive company-hosted events.

## **Why Content Pillars Matter**

Content pillars:

1. **Simplify Content Creation:** Provide a clear structure for brainstorming and developing ideas that stay aligned with your goals.

2. **Strengthen Your Employer Brand:** Ensure consistency in messaging across different touchpoints.

3. **Target the Right Audience at the Right Time:** Match the type of content to the mindset of your audience in their respective stages of the TJIE.

To make content pillars work effectively:

○ **Stick to Your Strategy:** Every piece of content must align with your Key Story Themes and desired employer brand perceptions.

○ **Prioritize the Talent's Journey and Their Challenges, Pain Points, Desires, and Aspirations During the Journey:** Ensure the content resonates with where your audience is in their journey.

○ **Keep it Balanced:** Avoid overloading one pillar at the expense of others, maintaining harmony between aspirational, professional, and emotional content.

In the following chapters, we'll dive deeper into each of the content pillars, providing practical guidance and examples for applying them in your employer branding efforts.

## CHAPTER 15

# Pillar One:
# The Aspirational Bridge

*"People don't buy
what you do; they
buy why you do it."*

SIMON SINEK

Pillar One content is the heart and soul of your employer branding strategy. It builds the first layer of trust, familiarity, and connection with your target audience. This pillar isn't about roles, responsibilities, or job postings. It's about creating an aspirational bridge that connects your organization's personality with your audience's desires, dreams, and values.

If your employer brand were a person, Pillar One would be their warm handshake, friendly smile, and engaging first conversation. It's the gateway to your audience's curiosity and interest, paving the way for deeper engagement and long-term loyalty.

## What is Pillar One?

Pillar One content combines the winning sustainable attention and growing employer awareness phases of the Talent Journey of the Information Era™ (TJIE). It is the most extensive content pillar in The Magnetic Employer Branding Method™, typically encompassing 60 to 70 percent of your total employer brand content.

The goal? To build an emotional connection by showing your audience how your organization's values, beliefs, and purpose align with their aspirations for a better life. Pillar One content focuses on who you are as an organization—not what you do.

## *Key Characteristics of Pillar One Content*

1. **Human-Centric:** Focus on your target audience, their aspirations, and their life goals. Show them they are the hero of the story, not your organization.
2. **Aspirational:** Highlight how your organization contributes to a better life for its people, customers, and society.
3. **Relatable:** Share stories, values, and insights that resonate with shared human experiences.
4. **Lifestyle-Oriented:** Position your organization as more than a workplace—a community, a support system, and a values-driven ecosystem.

Here's how you can create compelling content that fits Pillar One:

### 1. Organizational Values in Action

- **Post:** "Why we believe kindness is the greatest strength a leader can have—stories from our people."
- **Format:** Short video interviews or carousel posts showcasing employees' experiences with leadership kindness.
### 2. Aspirational Quotes and Reflections
- **Post:** "On Fridays, we reflect on what inspires us. Today, our CEO shares their favorite quote: 'Leadership is not about being in charge. It's

about taking care of those in your charge.' –
Simon Sinek."

- **Format:** Beautifully designed quote graphics
for Instagram or LinkedIn with a short
accompanying story.

### 3. Community and Connection

- **Post:** "Behind every great team is a community
that supports one another. Here's how our
employees are building connections that go
beyond work."
- **Format:** A candid reel or photo carousel
capturing moments from a recent internal event
or team-building activity.

### 4. Myth-Busting and Fun Content

- **Post:** "We busted five myths about our industry
that even our team believed when they joined us.
Which one surprises you the most?"
- **Format:** Engaging carousel post or meme series.

## Crafting Pillar One Content: The "Better Life" Approach

The essence of Pillar One content is showing your audience
how life with your organization contributes to a better life
for them. This doesn't mean promising perks like gym
memberships or free coffee. Instead, it's about aligning your
organizational purpose and culture with their aspirations.

Imagine your organization as a person enjoying a drink with a potential hire. What values, beliefs, and stories would come up in a casual, meaningful conversation? Use this mindset to create content that inspires and resonates.

## *Best Practices for Pillar One Content Creation*

**Know Your Audience's Aspirations:** Use insights from your Magnetic Employer Brand Strategy to pinpoint what drives your target audience. Are they looking for professional growth, work-life balance, or a sense of purpose? What values do they hold near?

**Leverage Key Story Themes:** Your Key Story Themes serve as content categories for this pillar. Each theme offers countless angles and stories to explore.

**Involve Your People:** Authentic stories and comments in the forms of quotes from employees and management provide the credibility and relatability that audiences crave. Feature their individual voices prominently.

**Embrace Visual Storytelling:** Use candid photos, short videos, and authentic graphics that capture the human essence of your organization. Avoid stock images—they're a shortcut to irrelevance.

**Maintain Consistency:** Stay true to your desired employer brand perceptions in every post. Consistent messaging builds trust and makes your audience feel they understand who you are.

## Content Ideas for Pillar One

Here's a collection of content ideas designed to spark connection with your target audience through relatable, thought-provoking, and inspiring content. When you create Pillar One Content, think about your organization if it was a person. Your company values, beliefs, ways of work (your culture), purpose, key areas of focus, goals, objectives and your mission and vision represent those of your Organization Person.

### #1 Beliefs and Values

**Key Message:** "Success isn't just about hard work; it's about working with purpose and aligning your actions with your core values."

**Ideal Formats:**

- **Visual Post**: A motivational quote graphic ("Align your grind with your mind.")
- **Microblog**: A short story reflecting on why staying true to values is key to success.
- **Carousel**: Steps to identify and align personal values with daily actions.

### #2 Lifestyle Aspirations

**Key Message:** "Creating balance in life is about embracing small, meaningful moments that build joy daily."

**Ideal Formats:**

- **Reels/Short Videos:** A montage showing morning routines or hobbies that bring joy.
- **Interactive Poll:** "What's your favorite way to recharge during the weekend?"
- **Carousel:** Tips to design a work-life balance that aligns with personal priorities.

### #3 Career Aspirations

**Key Message:** "Your dream career isn't found—it's built by embracing the journey and the lessons along the way."

**Ideal Formats:**

- **Personal Reflection Post**: A story about someone turning a small role into a big opportunity.
- **How-To Guide:** "5 Ways to Gain Clarity on Your Career Goals."
- **Infographic**: Visual timeline of how long-term goals are built step-by-step.

### #4 Celebrating Achievements

**Key Message:** "Every small win is a step toward greatness—let's cheer for progress over perfection."

**Ideal Formats:**

- **Story Highlight**: Audience submissions of small daily wins.

- **Reel**: "3 Small Wins I'm Celebrating This Week (and you should too!)."
- **Interactive Post**: "What's one win you're proud of this week? Share in the comments!"

## #5 Trials and Tribulations (Overcoming Challenges)

**Key Message:** "Every challenge we overcome becomes a chapter in our growth story."

**Ideal Formats:**

- **Text Post with Graphic:** "When was the last time you turned an obstacle into an opportunity?"
- **Video Testimonial:** Personal stories of facing challenges and lessons learned.
- **Infographic:** "The Growth Curve: How setbacks often precede breakthroughs."

*Go to 'What's next? Free Resources That Come with This Book' to download a PDF with additional Pillar One content ideas.*

## Why Pillar One Matters

Pillar One is where trust begins. It's how you make a lasting first impression and create an emotional resonance with your audience. When done well, this content becomes the foundation of your employer brand strategy, drawing your target audience closer, and keeping them engaged over the long term.

Remember, this pillar isn't about quick wins. It's about building relationships that last. Like all great relationships, it takes time, patience, and authenticity. In the end, the effort is worth it: a loyal, aspirational audience that sees your organization as a partner in their journey toward a better life.

## Conclusion: Bringing Pillar One to Life

Pillar One is the heartbeat of your employer branding strategy. It's where you spark curiosity, ignite aspirations, and begin to build the trust that transforms passive followers into an engaged audience. It's your opportunity to say, "We see you, we understand your dreams, and we're here to inspire and guide you."

But as with any creative endeavor, the magic of Pillar One lies in execution. To ensure your efforts resonate deeply and authentically, keep these guiding principles in mind:

## *1. Stay True to Your Audience's Aspirations*

When creating Pillar One content, remember: It's not about you—it's about them. Every piece of content should answer the question, "How does this speak to their dreams, challenges, or values?" Authenticity and empathy are your strongest tools. Avoid generic platitudes, and instead focus on creating moments of recognition, where your audience thinks, *They get me.*

Quick Tip: Use your Key Story Themes as your compass. They ground your content in your organization's values while connecting to your audience's hopes and goals.

## 2. Measure What Matters

While Pillar One content is more aspirational than transactional, you still need to track its performance to refine your strategy. Focus on metrics that reflect engagement and growing awareness:

- **Engagement:** Are people liking, sharing, commenting, or reacting to your content?

- **Audience Growth:** Are you steadily gaining followers or subscribers within your target audience?

- **Sentiment:** Are your audience's responses positive and enthusiastic?

These indicators show whether your content is connecting emotionally with your audience. Remember, success here isn't measured by immediate action, but by building a foundation of trust and attention.

## 3. Avoid the Pitfalls

Even the best intentions can go astray. Here are some common missteps to avoid:

- **Overly Corporate Tone:** Keep it conversational and human. If it sounds like a press release, it will fail to connect.
- **Brand-Centric Focus:** Avoid talking about your company. Instead, show how your values, morals, ethics, and purpose align with theirs through storytelling and relatable scenarios.
- **Inconsistency:** Posting sporadically or mixing unrelated topics confuses your audience. Stick to your themes and maintain regularity.

Quick Tip: Develop an editorial calendar that aligns your content themes with audience needs throughout the year. Plan seasonal or timely content in advance.

## 4. Think Beyond the Post

Pillar One is your chance to experiment with formats and find creative ways to reach your audience. Don't limit yourself to static posts; consider:

- **Interactive Content:** Polls, quizzes, or "ask me anything" sessions spark two-way conversations.
- **User-Generated Stories:** Share content from employees, alumni, or audience members to create a community vibe.
- **Behind-the-Scenes Snippets:** Give your audience a glimpse of your culture, leadership, or work environment.

Pro Tip: Use your Key Story Themes as a creative springboard. For example, if your theme is "Empowering

STORY-DRIVEN EMPLOYER BRANDING

Professional Growth," create content like "Five Books That Changed the Way Our Team Thinks About Leadership."

## 5. Build Bridges, Not Campaigns

Pillar One isn't about creating one-off campaigns. It's about building a consistent narrative that becomes a bridge between your audience's aspirations and your employer brand. Think of it as a relationship, not a transaction.

**To make this easier, follow this simple framework:**

1. Choose one Key Story Theme.
2. Brainstorm three ideas that reflect your audience's values and align with the theme.
3. Draft your content with the audience as the hero of the story.
4. Share it with a focus on sparking conversation, not just attention.

Call to Action: "Take fifteen minutes right now to jot down three ideas for your Pillar One content based on one of your Key Story Themes. Don't overthink it—your first ideas are often the most authentic. Then, schedule a time to create and share one piece of content this week."

## 6. Remember the Long Game

Your Pillar One efforts won't go viral overnight, but that's not the point. You're laying the groundwork for something bigger: a Magnetic Employer Brand that attracts, inspires, and retains the right people for years to come.

As Seth Godin says, "The goal is to make the change happen and to do it in a way that you're proud of, that's worth talking about, and that lasts."

When you focus on creating value and emotional connection, your employer brand becomes not just a presence in their feeds but a meaningful part of their lives. That's the real power of Pillar One.

Let's dive into the next pillar to keep building on your masterpiece!

## CHAPTER 16

# Pillar Two: Building Aspirational Connections with Your Business

*"Work is not just about earning a paycheck; it's about doing something that enriches your life and aligns with your purpose."*

SHERYL SANDBERG

I f Pillar One content is about attracting attention and creating a connection on shared values and lifestyle aspirations, Pillar Two is where you begin to introduce your audience to the professional and organizational dimensions of your employer brand. This is the stage where your audience starts to see your company not just as relatable, but as a destination—a place where they can grow, contribute, and thrive professionally.

Think of Pillar Two as the bridge between personal aspirations and professional ambitions. Your audience, having felt the emotional resonance of your brand in Pillar One, is now ready to engage with the deeper narrative of what your company stands for and what it offers in terms of career potential and business value.

## The Purpose of Pillar Two Content

The purpose of Pillar Two is to:

1. **Establish your company as a professional destination.** Showcase your expertise, your industry leadership, and your innovative spirit in ways that captivate the curiosity of your audience.

2. **Highlight career possibilities.** Without turning into job ads, this pillar offers glimpses of what it means and looks like to work at your company— what makes it exciting, challenging, and meaningful for your people, including team leads, managers, and top management.

3. **Nurture an aspirational connection.** You're not just saying, "Work here." You're messaging, "This is the kind of place where someone like you could thrive."

4. **Build trust in your business and its people.** By showcasing the human side of your expertise—through leadership voices, employee stories, and thought leadership—you invite your audience to see the soul and knowledge behind the strategy.

## What Makes Pillar Two Unique?

Unlike Pillar One, where the focus is on creating a shared emotional foundation, Pillar Two dives into the professional "why." Why should someone choose to work for your organization—not just in general, but as a deliberate step in their career?

**Here's how Pillar Two content differentiates itself:**

### 1. It's professional but still human

While showcasing your business, avoid corporate jargon or faceless messaging. Keep it relatable, approachable, and authentic. Include both perspectives: the corporate and the employee.

### 2. It's informative but aspirational

Share tangible facts and insights about your business while painting a vision of what it's like to be part of the journey.

### 3. It transitions focus subtly

This content pivots from "It's about them" (in Pillar One) to "Here's why we might be a great match."

## Examples of Pillar Two Content

### Leadership Perspectives:

Share insights from your leadership team on industry trends, company vision, and the future of your field. This positions your company as a thought leader while giving your audience a sense of who they'd be working under.

Example: A LinkedIn post from your CEO discussing the future of clean energy and how your company is leading the charge with innovation and bold ideas.

### Hero Career Stories™:

Feature stories of employees who have thrived in your organization, highlighting their journeys and growth through challenges and obstacles to win the day.

Example: A blog post or video about a mid-level engineer who grew into a leadership role despite going through a personally challenging period in their life, supported by the company's mentoring program and a caring mentor or team leader.

### Values in Action:

Showcase how your values come to life in real-world business decisions, projects, or client work.

Example: A behind-the-scenes look at a project where your company prioritized sustainability over short-term profits, aligning with your core belief in long-term responsibility.

**Educational Thought Leadership:**

Share industry insights, professional tips, or how-to guides that establish your company as a knowledge hub for your field.

Example: An infographic or white paper on trends shaping your industry, authored by your internal experts.

**Showcasing Business Innovation:**

Highlight the cutting-edge work your company does, showing how it aligns with broader societal or industry shifts.

Example: A short video showing how your company leverages AI to solve real-world challenges in logistics.

**Cultural Testimonials:**

Show how your culture empowers employees to bring their best selves to work.

Example: A photo carousel on Instagram featuring employees sharing their favorite aspect of the company culture, with quotes and authentic snapshots.

## How Pillar Two Aligns with Key Story Themes

Pillar Two content must always reflect your Key Story Themes. Here's how to integrate them effectively:

**1. Relate Every Story Back to the Theme:**

Each piece of content should support at least one Key Story Theme, ensuring your messaging remains cohesive.

Example: If a Key Story Theme is "Empowering Professional Growth," your Hero Career Stories™ should highlight the opportunities and resources your company provides for career development.

**2. Balance the Company and Employee Perspective:**

Each story should be balanced between the company's narrative (what you do, why you do it) and the employee's experience (how it feels to be part of it). While these can be brought into the same piece of content, it is generally more impactful to provide both perspectives as separate pieces of content but linked with each other.

Example: A blog post and social media carousel together could combine an overview of a groundbreaking project with quotes from team members about the pride they felt contributing to it.

# Practical Tips for Creating Pillar Two Content

### Leverage Employee Voices:

Your employees are your most credible storytellers. Use their words, tones of voice, faces, and experiences to give authenticity to your brand.

### Diversify Content Formats:

Experiment with blogs, short-form videos, infographics, and carousels to engage your audience in different ways.

### Stay True to Your Employer Brand Perceptions:

Every piece of content should subtly reinforce the perceptions you want your audience to associate with your brand. Creating series from the same content idea is a great way to reinforce both the desired perception and the Key Story Theme.

### Invite Interaction:

End content with a question or call to action that encourages engagement, such as comments, shares, or even direct messages.

### Test and Iterate:

Monitor with analytics which types of content resonate most with your audience and refine your approach over time.

## The Power of Planting Aspirational Seeds

Pillar Two content is where your employer brand evolves from a warm handshake to a professional introduction. It's the phase where your audience begins to envision not just who you are, but how they might fit into your story. This is the content that cultivates curiosity and builds anticipation. It's the moment where you plant the seeds of aspiration— seeds that, with consistent care, will grow into a connection so strong that your company becomes synonymous with their professional dreams.

But here's the secret: Pillar Two isn't about rushing the journey. It's not about immediately converting someone into an applicant or employee. Instead, it's about building the foundation of trust and admiration, so when they do make a move, you're already in their hearts and minds as their employer of choice.

## The "Magnetic" Outcome of Pillar Two: Here's Why it Works

When done right, Pillar Two content turns casual observers into career aspirants. It cultivates trust, admiration, and professional curiosity, leaving your audience thinking, *This is a company I could see myself growing with—maybe not today, but someday.* Here's what makes it magnetic:

**It nurtures professional ambition.**

Your content doesn't just tell them what you do; it shows them how being part of your company can elevate their career, skills, and sense of purpose. It's like giving them a sneak peek of what it feels like to grow with you.

**It respects the long game.**

Career decisions are deeply personal and often take years to unfold. Pillar Two is about playing the long game—being present and consistent, so when the timing is right for them, your company is the obvious choice.

**It builds loyalty before the hire.**

By sharing stories, insights, and experiences that align with their aspirations, you create an emotional connection that endures even if they're not ready to act immediately. They might not apply today, but they'll root for your company, share your content, and recommend you to their peers.

**It transforms your reputation.**

Think about the companies that have captured your admiration without ever selling to you directly. That's the kind of influence Pillar Two content creates—it turns your company into a beacon of trust and inspiration in your field.

## A Vision for the Future

Imagine this: A professional in your target audience—let's call her Anna—stumbles upon a LinkedIn post where one of your team members shares their growth journey at your company. Anna is intrigued. She follows your page, engages with more content, and begins to associate your brand with her own professional ambitions. Months pass, and she isn't actively looking for a new role, but your content keeps appearing, reinforcing that connection. One day, an opportunity opens in your company. Anna doesn't just apply—she does so with confidence and excitement because your brand already feels like home.

That's the power of Pillar Two. It's not transactional. It's transformational.

## Closing Thoughts

Here's the truth: Employer branding is about creating bridges, not barriers. This pillar isn't about "selling" your company; it's about inviting the right people to see themselves in your story—to picture a future where they thrive alongside you.

Think of it this way: If Pillar One is where you meet and connect with someone at a casual café, Pillar Two is where you sit down for a deeper chat, talking about shared dreams, aspirations, and goals. It's not about bragging or pitching; it's about saying, "This is what excites us—could it excite you, too?"

When you create content for this pillar, imagine you're talking to someone who's curious but hesitant—someone who needs that little nudge to lean in closer. Share what truly sets your company apart, not in a "we're the best" kind of way but with sincerity and substance. This is your chance to lead with your values, inspire trust, and give them a reason to bookmark your name in their mental list of dream employers.

Remember, it's not about trying to attract everyone; it's about connecting deeply with the right ones. And when you approach it with authenticity and purpose, you're not just building an audience—you're creating a community of future colleagues who can't wait to be part of your journey. When you master Pillar Two, you're not just creating content; you're cultivating a future workforce of advocates, believers, and change-makers. By the time they're ready to make their move, the decision won't feel like a leap of faith—it will feel like coming home.

So go ahead and dare to be magnetic.

Ready to move to Pillar Three?

## CHAPTER 17

# Pillar Three: Strengthening Connection and Loyalty

*"When people go to work, they shouldn't have to leave their hearts at home."*

BETTY BENDER

Pillar Three is the heart of your employer branding efforts. While Pillar One attracts attention and Pillar Two builds professional credibility, Pillar Three captures the hearts and creates deep emotional connections, camaraderie, and loyalty. This is where your organization becomes more than a workplace: a tribe and a place where shared values and collective pride turn employees into ambassadors and external audiences into advocates and raving fans.

This pillar showcases the human side of your organization—the stories, traditions, and experiences that make your people proud to be part of your journey. It's where you show your audience what it feels like to be part of your tribe, to walk alongside you in pursuit of something meaningful.

It's not just about the work but the camaraderie, the shared values, and the moments of pride that make your organization more than just a workplace—that magnetic pull that fosters a sense of belonging for those within and aspiration for those outside.

## How Pillar Three Aligns with Key Story Themes

Your Key Story Themes act as the foundation for crafting content under Pillar Three. They ensure that every story, celebration, and behind-the-scenes moment reflects your desired employer brand perceptions.

For example:

If one of your Key Story Themes is **Empowering Professional Growth**, Pillar Three might include stories about mentorship moments, career transformations, or how teams collaborate to achieve ambitious goals.

If your Key Story Theme is **Creating Tangible Impact on Sustainability**, this pillar could feature employee-driven sustainability projects, personal accounts of making a difference, or team efforts to innovate green solutions.

For a theme like **Driving the Clean Energy Revolution**, Pillar Three could showcase team stories about overcoming challenges, celebrating milestones in innovation, or spotlighting the pride of contributing to something transformative.

By aligning your content with these themes, you create a cohesive narrative that amplifies your employer brand and deeply resonates with your audience.

## Practical Tips for Creating Pillar Three Content

Creating content that resonates deeply requires intention and creativity. Here are some practical tips:

### 1. Dig for Personal Stories:

Find those moments that reflect individual growth, teamwork, or cultural values. These could be stories of resilience, a career breakthrough, or a team's unique way of celebrating success.

### 2. Invite Employees into the Process:

Host workshops or casual conversations where employees can share their proudest moments or what makes them

STORY-DRIVEN EMPLOYER BRANDING

feel connected to your company. This provides authentic material straight from the source.

### 3. Create Multi-Dimensional Content:

Combine personal narratives with broader cultural insights. For instance, pair a story about an employee's career journey with a note on how your leadership principles supported that growth.

### 4. Use Visuals to Amplify Emotion:

A photo of a team cheering during a project launch or a video capturing the excitement of an event can convey more emotion than words alone.

### 5. Celebrate the Everyday Wins:

It doesn't always have to be about major milestones. Highlighting small, meaningful moments can be just as impactful—like an intern's first big presentation or a team potluck that strengthened connections.

## *Examples of Pillar Three Content*

- **Employee Spotlights:** Share stories that highlight personal growth or team camaraderie, such as, "How Alex found a mentor who changed their career trajectory."
- **Team Achievements:** Celebrate milestones with content like, "Here's how our team turned a challenge into an innovation."

- **Behind-the-Scenes Glimpses:** Offer exclusive peeks into cultural events or unique workplace rituals, like, "A Day in the life of our creative team."

- **Alumni Features:** Keep the tribe spirit alive with stories like, "Where are they now? Celebrating the continued success of our alumni."

- **Moments of Gratitude:** Shine a spotlight on acts of kindness, teamwork, or leadership within the company, such as, "How our people stepped up to support a colleague in need."

## Here's What Makes Pillar Three Magnetic

Pillar Three works because it taps into the emotional core of your target audience. People don't just want a job; they want a purpose. They want to feel proud of where they work and the people they work with. Here's why this pillar has a magnetic pull:

- **Authenticity Breeds Trust:** When employees share their real stories, it creates trust and relatability. External audiences see these moments as genuine, making your employer brand stand out in a sea of generic corporate messaging.

- **Belonging Creates Loyalty:** When your content fosters a sense of community, it deepens loyalty among employees and inspires external audiences to imagine themselves as part of that community.

- **Stories Spark Advocacy:** Employees who feel connected and valued are more likely to share these moments with their networks, organically amplifying your employer brand.

When you focus on Pillar Three, your organization becomes more than just an employer—it becomes a community. Employees feel valued and proud, creating a sense of loyalty that extends beyond their tenure. They naturally share their experiences with their networks, amplifying your employer brand's reach through authentic advocacy.

At the same time, external audiences see a workplace where people thrive emotionally and professionally. They start imagining themselves as part of your team, aligning with your purpose, and contributing to something greater than themselves.

Pillar Three is where the magic of employer branding truly happens. It's the stories, the connections, and the moments that make people proud to be part of your organization— and inspire others to want to join.

When you're working on this pillar, I want you to think about the stories you'd tell at a reunion. What are the moments that define your time with a team? What would make you smile, tear up, or feel a rush of pride? Those are the stories your target audience wants to hear.

Make this pillar personal. Lean into the moments that make your organization truly unique. Share the pride, the struggles, the joy, and the victories. Because in the end, employer branding is about people, and people connect through stories. Here's the beauty of it: When you focus on creating those moments and sharing them authentically, you're not just branding—you're building a legacy.

## CHAPTER 18

# Content Plan: Transforming Strategy into Action

*"Give me six hours to chop down a tree, and I will spend the first four sharpening the axe."*

WIDELY ATTRIBUTED TO
ABRAHAM LINCOLN

Imagine standing at the start of a marathon without a map, unsure of the course, and hoping sheer enthusiasm will carry you to the finish line. Sounds absurd, doesn't it? Yet, this is exactly what it feels like when you approach employer branding without a content plan. A well-structured content plan isn't just a nice-to-have—it's your road map, your toolkit, and your safety net. It ensures that your employer branding efforts are systematic, efficient, and scalable, helping you achieve your goals while avoiding chaos or burnout.

But let's be real: It's not enough to plan. You need a plan that works. A plan so systematic and compelling that it becomes second nature to your team—a well-oiled machine generating a steady stream of content that aligns with your strategy, engages your audience, and delivers real results.

Let's dive into how you can create a content plan that doesn't just function but thrives, giving your Magnetic Employer Branding Method™ the momentum it deserves.

## Why a Content Plan is Non-Negotiable

Your Magnetic Employer Brand won't build itself. Without a content plan:

1. **Consistency Falters:** Sporadic posting sends a message of inconsistency—exactly what you don't want associated with your employer brand.
2. **Relevance Wanes:** Without structure, you risk veering offtrack, creating content that doesn't serve your audience or align with your Key Story Themes.

3. **Opportunity is Missed:** A lack of planning leaves you scrambling for ideas, undermining your ability to connect meaningfully with your audience.

Your content plan is your insurance policy against these pitfalls. It's what transforms ideas into action, ensuring your brand message is delivered consistently, strategically, and memorably.

## The Five Steps to Systematic Content Planning and Marketing

### 1. Plan and Schedule with Purpose

Planning begins with your Key Story Themes. These are your content pillars, the foundation of your employer branding narrative. Use them to structure your plan, ensuring all themes are evenly represented.

- **Incorporate Pillars:** Align your plan with the three content pillars, ensuring you address every phase of the Talent Journey.
- **Account for Events:** Add posts for recruitment drives, organizational milestones, or strategic campaigns to ensure your content stays timely and relevant.

Pro Tip: Use tools like Trello or Asana to visually organize your content plan, assign tasks, and monitor progress in real time.

## 2. Ideate Content That Resonates

Content ideation is where the magic begins. Involve your employees, stakeholders, and even generative AI to build a backlog of raw ideas.

- **Facilitate Ideation Workshops:** Host sessions focused on specific Key Story Themes with diverse groups from your organization.

- **Leverage AI and Trends:** Use tools like ChatGPT to generate fresh ideas or adapt trending topics to suit your employer branding strategy.

- **Check out Your Content Data From Your Website and Social Media:** Evaluate what type of content seems to have worked the best with your existing audience. Just make sure your existing audience matches with who you aim to target with this strategy.

## 3. Create and Produce Content in Batches

Efficiency is the name of the game. Content creation is time-consuming, but batching your efforts ensures you're always ahead.

- **Batch Production:** Dedicate specific times to create multiple pieces of content, so you're never scrambling.

- **Raw Information Gathering:** Collect testimonials, visuals, or insights that can be woven into compelling stories.

- **Publication-Ready Content:** Each post should have polished copy, hashtags, links, and visuals ready to go.

Tools: Platforms like Canva Pro, Riverside.fm, and CapCut make it easier to create high-quality visuals and videos.

## 4. Publish and Promote Strategically

Your content's success depends not just on what you post but how and when you post it.

- **Automate Publishing:** Tools like Buffer or Later allow you to schedule posts at optimal times for maximum reach.
- **Optimize Timing:** Analyze platform algorithms to post when your audience is most active.

## 5. Engage and Refine

Posting isn't the end of the process—it's the beginning of a conversation. Social media thrives on interaction, and so should you.

- **Engage Proactively:** Respond to comments, start discussions, and build relationships with your audience.
- **Analyze Performance:** Use analytics tools like Metricool to track reach, engagement, and conversions. Identify patterns and adapt your strategy to amplify what works.

## The Role of Visuals in Your Content Plan

Humans are visual creatures—half of our brain is wired to process images. A compelling visual can communicate your employer brand's message in a second, making it an essential part of your content strategy.

**Four Key Types of Visuals**

1. **Casual Portraits:** Showcase real people, real moments.
2. **Candid Photos:** Capture authentic, unscripted interactions.
3. **Collaborative Scenes:** Highlight teamwork and camaraderie.
4. **Timeless Imagery:** Use evergreen visuals that stay relevant.

"Show, don't tell" is more than a mantra—it's the backbone of effective branding. Pair your written messages with visuals that reinforce and amplify them.

Tip: I have created a PDF called "Quick Tips for Creating and Maintaining Your Employer Brand Photo Bank." Find the link in the Resources section of this book.

## Simplifying the Content Creation Process

The best processes are repeatable. Here's a streamlined approach to creating employer branding content:

- **Curate Relevant Content:** Share news, insights, or studies from credible sources that align with your themes.

- **Repurpose and Recycle:** Adapt successful posts into new formats or lengths to extend their life and reach.

- **Collaborate with Influencers:** Partner with internal and external (B2B thought leaders for co-branded content.

- **Bundle and Schedule:** Plan and prepare content in advance to ensure consistency and efficiency.

## Why the Magnetic Content Plan Works

This process isn't just about organization—it's about transformation. A systematic content plan empowers you to:

1. **Stay Strategic:** Every post aligns with your desired employer brand perceptions.
2. **Be Consistent:** Your audience knows what to expect, building trust and familiarity.
3. **Optimize Resources:** A clear plan reduces wasted effort and maximizes impact.

The result? A Magnetic Employer Brand that not only attracts talent but resonates deeply, creating a loyal following that aligns with your organization's vision and values.

## Closing Thoughts: Your Employer Brand is a Movement

Imagine your employer brand as a symphony, each piece of content a note that builds toward a harmonious whole. Without a conductor—a content plan—it's just noise. But with a plan, you create music.

This isn't about churning out content for the sake of it. It's about telling a story—your story—in a way that captivates, connects, and converts. So, take the time to craft your plan. Treat it as the foundation of your brand's legacy. Because when you get it right, your employer brand doesn't just support your organization—it elevates it. And that, my friend, is the ultimate win.

# ENSURING ROI: SUSTAINING YOUR MAGNETIC EMPLOYER BRAND

## CHAPTER 19

# Data-Driven Assessment of Your Employer Branding Efforts

> "In God we trust. All others must bring data."

MARY WALTON

W hy does data-driven assessment matter? Think of data-driven assessment as your employer branding GPS—it ensures you're heading in the right direction, highlights when you veer off course, and helps you reach your destination efficiently.

Without regular checks, you might be investing effort in areas that don't deliver the intended impact or ROI. And here's the kicker: You might not even realize it. By embracing a data-driven approach, you can confidently demonstrate progress, adjust strategies, and showcase tangible value to stakeholders.

## Step 1: Build the Foundation— What to Measure

Start by tying your assessment efforts back to your Master Plan. Here are the key areas to evaluate:

- **Content Performance:** Track likes, shares, comments, and saves on social media posts. Are they engaging your target audience? Look for patterns in high-performing content and replicate the winning formula.

- **Audience Growth:** Monitor metrics like follower growth, email subscribers, or members of your talent pool. Are your awareness-building efforts drawing the right people into your orbit?

- **Engagement Over Time:** Measure the depth of interactions with your content. High engagement levels—such as thoughtful comments or shares—indicate a stronger connection with your audience.

- **Goal-Specific KPIs:** Go back to the KPIs defined in your strategy.

## Step 2: Establish a Routine— How and When to Assess

Effective assessment is about regularity and simplicity. Implement a three-tiered evaluation routine:

1. **Monthly Metrics Review:** Track performance of individual posts, identify trends, and fine-tune your tactics.
2. **Quarterly Strategy Check-in:** Evaluate your KPIs and broader campaign outcomes. Are you moving closer to your strategic goals?
3. **Annual Impact Analysis:** Measure the long-term effects of your employer branding efforts, such as reductions in recruitment costs or improved employee satisfaction scores.

## Step 3: Tools for the Trade

Here's a quick rundown of tools to simplify and elevate your assessment:

- **Social Media Analytics:** LinkedIn, Instagram, Facebook, YouTube, and TikTok all provide native insights.

- **All-in-One Platforms:** Tools like Sprout Social, Buffer, and Metricool consolidate performance data across channels.
- **Surveys and Feedback:** Tools like Typeform or Google Forms can collect qualitative insights from employees and candidates.

## Step 4: Qualitative Matters— The Human Element

Data tells one side of the story; qualitative feedback completes it.

- **Employee Check-ins:** Use surveys to ask employees about their perceptions of your brand and how they feel about being part of the organization.
- **Candidate Experience Surveys:** What are applicants saying about your hiring process? Their experiences can highlight potential gaps in your employer brand alignment.

## Actionable Insights

When you notice certain metrics underperforming, ask:

- Is the content aligned with my Key Story Themes?
- Are we speaking to the right audience?
- Have external factors shifted audience behavior?

## CHAPTER 20

# Ongoing Actions to Maintain Your Magnetic Employer Brand

"*Success is never owned,
it's rented—and the
rent is due every day.*"

RORY VADEN

W hy is continuous action non-negotiable? Building your employer brand is not a "set it and forget it" initiative. It's a marathon that requires regular effort to sustain momentum. Much like a garden, if you stop watering and nurturing it, weeds will take over. The ongoing actions outlined here ensure your employer brand doesn't just survive but thrives.

## Aligning Actions with Your Master Plan

Revisit your strategy regularly to ensure alignment. The employer branding landscape evolves, and so do your company's priorities. Staying nimble is key.

## *Ongoing Actions to Implement*

### 1. Keep Content Fresh and Relevant

- Update your Key Story Themes with fresh angles. For instance, if your business launches a new sustainability initiative, integrate it into your content.

- Leverage trending topics when they align with your brand. For example, global discussions about work-life balance can highlight your company's flexible working policies.

### 2. Engage With Your Audience

- Spend time in the comment sections of your posts. Respond authentically to comments and build conversations.

- Don't just post and ghost—engage. Actively comment on posts by industry thought leaders, alumni, and potential candidates to build visibility and trust.

**3. Encourage Employee Advocacy**
- Launch an internal advocacy program that rewards employees for sharing authentic stories about their work.
- Create branded templates or suggest ideas to make participation easy.

**4. Monitor the Competition**
- Regularly review the employer branding efforts of your competitors. What's working for them, and how can you differentiate?
- Tools like Brandwatch or Mention can help monitor conversations and sentiment in your industry.

**5. Host Employer Branding Checkpoints**
- Schedule internal meetings to discuss progress and share insights. Celebrate wins, no matter how small.

## *The Power of Periodic Adjustments*

Think of this as steering a ship. Minor course corrections can keep you on track to your destination. Conducting quarterly review workshops with your employer branding team ensures everyone remains aligned and motivated.

STORY-DRIVEN EMPLOYER BRANDING

## The Magnetic Outcome of ROI Accountability

### A Clearer Path to ROI

When you track and assess your employer branding efforts consistently:

- You identify what works—and what doesn't—so you can invest resources wisely.
- You build credibility and trust with internal stakeholders, showing them the tangible impact of your work.
- You future-proof your employer brand by staying agile and relevant.

### A Personal Reflection

Think of ROI assessment not as a burden but as your opportunity to showcase your incredible work. Every data point, every piece of feedback, is a badge of honor that says, "You're making a difference." Your employer branding strategy is not just a plan—it's a dynamic, evolving story that you have the privilege to tell.

### Closing Thoughts

As we wrap up this section, remember: ROI is the culmination of your commitment. It's proof that the time, energy, and resources invested in your employer brand have real, measurable value.

With consistent assessment and ongoing action, you're not just building an employer brand—you're crafting a legacy that elevates your company and the careers of those who choose to be part of it.

# CONCLUSION

*"Attention is currency."*

GARY VAYNERCHUK

I n today's hyper-connected, information-driven world, capturing and sustaining attention is the greatest challenge—and the greatest opportunity. Through this book, we've explored a transformative approach to employer branding that goes beyond campaigns and surface-level messaging. We've journeyed together through the Talent Journey of the Information Era™, unveiling the framework, tools, and mindset to turn your organization into a magnet for the right talent.

At its heart, The Magnetic Employer Branding Method™ is a paradigm shift. It's not about quick wins or superficial fixes; it's about creating deep, meaningful connections that align your company's values, culture, and goals with the aspirations of your ideal talent audience. It's about building trust, cultivating relationships, and creating an emotional pull that makes your brand irresistible.

## What You've Learned

Throughout this book, you've been introduced to a revolutionary approach to employer branding—The Magnetic Employer Branding Method™—designed to align your strategic company culture, employee experiences, and storytelling into a cohesive, irresistible magnet for top talent.

## *1. It All Starts with the Master Plan*

Every magnetic brand begins with a Master Plan, a strategic blueprint that defines your transformative employer branding mission, key goals, objectives, and the KPIs to measure your success, your strategic employer brand's target audience, desired employer brand perceptions, and Key Story Themes.

At its heart, the Master Plan is what separates organizations that dabble in employer branding from those that dominate the talent market. It's the guiding framework that ensures your efforts are not just consistent but strategic. It helps you:

- Define your goals and objectives with clarity.
- Connect your employer branding activities directly to business outcomes.
- Align every campaign, message, and touchpoint to your overarching strategy.
- Measure what matters and continuously refine your efforts for greater ROI.

This isn't just a plan—it's your playbook for success.

Without a plan, you're simply throwing ideas into the void. With it, you're orchestrating a masterpiece where every action and message serves a greater purpose—delivering real return on investment for your employer branding efforts.

The Master Plan is where you shift from being reactive to proactive. It's your North Star, ensuring you make intentional, data-driven decisions that resonate deeply with your target audience.

Remember: Random acts of talent marketing are just noise, but a Master Plan builds a symphony.

## 2. Strategic Company Culture: Your Differentiating DNA

Your company culture isn't just about fun perks or casual Fridays; it's the strategic engine that connects your business goals with the way your people work and lead.

A well-defined Strategic Company Culture sets the stage for authentic employer branding, ensuring your message reflects the reality of working at your organization—not just wishful thinking.

## 3. Employee and Candidate Experiences: The Proof of Your Brand

As the living, breathing testament of your brand's promises, employee experiences provide the stories that make your brand credible. Pair this with seamless candidate experiences, and you create a feedback loop of trust and advocacy that fuels your employer brand's authenticity.

## 4. Key Story Themes: The Magic Ingredient

These overarching narrative themes bring your brand's personality to life. They connect your culture, experiences, and values into stories that engage, inspire, and motivate your target talent audience.

Key Story Themes act as the creative scaffolding for all your employer branding efforts, ensuring consistency and relevance in cementing your desired employer brand perceptions.

## 5. The Talent Journey of the Information Era™

Your employer brand is built step-by-step through the Talent Journey. Each phase—from winning sustainable attention to growing employer awareness, cultivating employer brand affinity, and ultimately converting employer brand value— is carefully designed to guide talent from casual observers to committed employees who align with your mission and culture and contribute to the success of your business.

## 6. Content Pillars and Strategic Content Planning

A strong employer brand requires a systematic, strategic approach to content creation. The three content pillars ensure your messaging supports every phase of the Talent Journey, balancing short-term engagement with long-term loyalty. Content planning elevates your efforts, turning scattered ideas into a powerful narrative machine.

## 7. Performance and ROI

Employer branding is a business strategy, not a vanity project. By regularly assessing your performance through the KPIs defined in your Master Plan, you ensure your efforts translate into measurable impact—whether that's attracting top talent, reducing churn, or building a reputation as a truly magnetic employer.

## A Relationship Built on Trust and Authenticity

Employer branding is like dating. It starts with a first impression—your employer brand's "vibe." If that vibe is all about your company's needs, it's off-putting. But when it's about mutual interests, understanding, and connection, you build something lasting. As in any relationship, trust is the cornerstone. Without trust, there's no sustainable attention, no affinity, and no lasting value.

Through this book, we've likened the phases of employer branding to a relationship journey—from the initial spark of interest to the deep connection of shared values and commitment. And just as in relationships, authenticity and patience are everything. Rushing the process leads to misalignment and missed opportunities.

Take the first step by outlining your Master Plan. Reflect on your culture, your audience, and your goals. Build a foundation so solid, your brand will stand out even in the most competitive markets.

## Why You Need to Act Now

The talent market moves fast, and attention is a finite resource. Every day you delay is a day your competitors are building their brands, capturing attention, and forging connections with the talent you need. The world of work is evolving, and those who embrace this change will lead the way.

This isn't just about employer branding; it's about creating a workplace and a culture that reflect the best of who you are and what you stand for. It's about building a future where your organization isn't just a place to work—it's a place to belong, grow, and thrive.

# FINAL WORDS

T his book was not written to simply educate—it was written to inspire action, ignite change, and redefine what's possible in employer branding.

The journey doesn't end here. Together, let's transform how the world sees, feels, and experiences your brand.

Your Magnetic Employer Brand awaits.

With kindness and respect,

Susanna

# AFTERWORD

....................................................................................................

T hank you for taking the time to dive into this book and explore what it takes to build a Magnetic Employer Brand. I know your time is valuable, and the fact that you've chosen to invest it here means the world to me. More importantly, it tells me that you're ready to create meaningful change—not just in your workplace, but in the lives of the people who choose to be part of it.

I wrote this book not just because I believe in the power of employer branding, but because I see it as a bridge—a bridge that connects businesses and people in a way that creates a profound and lasting impact. Employer branding is not just about attracting talent. It's about crafting organizations where people—at every level—feel seen, valued, and inspired to give their best. It's about weaving together the stories, cultures, and experiences that unite those who own the business, those who run it, those who work there, and those who benefit from its work.

Through The Magnetic Employer Branding Method™, I hope to offer more than tools. I hope to inspire a vision where businesses operate as living, breathing communities, with clear strategies that align their ambitions with the human spirit. When strategic company cultures empower leaders and employees alike to work toward a shared purpose, they can achieve something extraordinary—not just for their organization, but for their customers, clients, stakeholders, and the world at large.

My mission is to unite businesses and people by showing that the greatest success lies in creating a win-win for everyone involved. Leaders who have clarity in their strategy and culture can inspire their teams to do incredible things. Employees who feel connected to their organization's values and mission can bring their whole selves to work, contributing to something bigger than themselves. And when these two forces align, they not only create a thriving workplace but also deliver greater good to society.

Yes, this mission is big. But I believe all big things are born in the hands of you, me, and those next to us. Greatness doesn't begin with monumental acts—it begins with small, meaningful steps. It starts with a leader who dares to align their culture with their vision, with a team that works together to bring stories to life, and with an organization that chooses to act authentically and strategically.

My hope is that this book gives you the tools, confidence, and inspiration to create your Magnetic Employer Brand—a brand that not only attracts talent but transforms lives. Together, we can build organizations where people thrive, leaders excel, and businesses create ripples of positive change far beyond their walls.

Let this be your starting point. Your Magnetic Employer Brand is waiting to be built. And the world is ready to be inspired by it. Let's create something extraordinary together.

# ACKNOWLEDGMENTS

Writing this book has been one of the most challenging yet rewarding journeys of my career. I couldn't have done it without the incredible support, inspiration, and guidance of so many people. Thank you to everyone who has walked this path with me—you've made this dream possible.

To my husband and business partner, **Leo**, thank you for believing in me and for always being my sounding board, cheerleader, and anchor. To my family, thank you for your endless patience, love, and support—you've been my haven through it all.

To **my brilliant teams and colleagues** at the former Heebo, and Employer Branding Agency Emine, thank you for the endless brainstorming sessions, your commitment to excellence, and for challenging me to always think bigger. This book is as much a reflection of your talent and dedication as it is of mine.

A special thank you to **Nora**, who stood by my side throughout this writing process, encouraging me and reminding me how much this book is needed and how much insight I have to share. You kept me from falling into impostor syndrome and instilled faith in my experience and knowledge. I'm forever grateful for your support, friendship, and loyalty.

To my best friends, **Elina** and **Terhi**, who, as authors yourselves, have been my greatest cheerleaders on this writing journey—your encouragement and unwavering support have meant the world to me.

To the pioneers in their respective fields, from whom I have learned so much, your work has been a guiding light for me. A special thank you to **Donald Miller of StoryBrand** for opening my eyes wide to the power of storytelling in marketing. To **the late Jack Welch**, who inspired me to become a business- and strategy-oriented HR professional when I was still finding my way in the field.

And to my former employer, **Olli Muurainen**, thank you for your inspiration as a successful entrepreneur and as an employer who gave me the freedom to "wing it" as an HR professional. You taught me so much about the symbiotic relationship between business and company culture. Thank you also for allowing me to adopt your phrase, "matching minds with mission." I am eternally grateful for your role in my journey.

Four special people also deserve to be mentioned:

**Susanna Paloheimo**, my Double Trouble, who stepped in as my sounding board, communication guru, connector, and even investor when I first became an entrepreneur. Despite all the ups and downs during our story, the ups are all I care to remember. I just want you to know: You are one of a kind, and I'm lucky to have you in my life.

**Marko Kulmala**, finding a friend in you has been nothing short of a blessing. Thank you for everything you are to me.

**Seppo Kuula**, my mentor, advisor, and friend throughout my entrepreneurial journey, your faith in me and my skills has formed the foundation of my confidence as an entrepreneur and businesswoman. Thank you for always having my back.

**Pekka Mattila**, you were meant to be here—pre-reading this book, writing the foreword, and guiding me through this journey and what comes after. You were my soulmate, my guide, and my biggest cheerleader. I trust you will guide me from heaven as you always did on earth. I miss you endlessly.

# AUTHOR BIO

**S**usanna Rantanen is an award-winning expert with over 20 years of experience driving business success through purpose-led company cultures, strategic HR, and employer branding. From accelerating growth through hiring, retention, and mergers & acquisitions to aligning talent strategies with business goals, Susanna's career is a testament to her ability to transform workplaces into engines of success.

Recognized as a **Thinkers360 Top 50 Global Thought Leader on Personal Branding in 2024** and one of the **Top 20 Women Leaders to Look Out For in 2024**, Susanna's expertise extends beyond strategy into storytelling and content marketing. She is the **Owner and Co-founder of Emine**, ranked as one of **Europe's Top 10 Employer Branding Agencies by HR Tech**, and the voice behind a **Top 3 Employer Branding podcast**, as voted by her listeners.

Susanna resides in beautiful Finland with her husband/business partner Leo and their son, Kasper and Maltipoo,

Luna. Together with her husband, they run Employer Branding Agency Emine located in Helsinki, Finland guiding modern-minded employer branding practitioners, business leaders and entrepreneurs apply story-driven employer branding for competitive advantage.

As the creator of The **Magnetic Employer Branding Method**™, Susanna has helped organizations worldwide match minds with missions to attract, engage, and retain top talent. Her work is grounded in the belief that aligning people with purpose and strategic company culture are the cornerstones of sustainable success.

Susanna's insights and methods are shaped by her journey as a purpose-driven leader, entrepreneur, and storyteller, making her a trusted guide for leaders and businesses ready to transform their employer brands into a strategic advantage.

# LEAVE A REVIEW

Thank you for reading or listening to my book. I really appreciate all of your feedback and love hearing what you have to say.

As a first-time book author, I need your input to make the next version of this book (and my future books) better and would love it if you could leave your honest review about this book.

Please take a minute now to leave a helpful review on Amazon letting me know what you thought of the book.

Thank you so much!

*Susanna*

# WHAT'S NEXT?

## Free Resources That Come with This Book

I have created for you additional free resources that hopefully inspire you to take action as you read or listen to this book. All of these extra resources are available for download on my website:

www.emine.fi/sdeb-free-resources

These resources include:

- The Master Plan template (pptx)
- The Talent Persona template (mentioned in Chapter 6)
- "Get started with identifying your Strategic Company Culture" (PDF)
- "Quick Tips for Creating and Maintaining Your Employer Brand Photo Bank"
- A PDF visualizing The Talent Journey of the Information Era™
- A PDF visualizing the employer brand story formula based on Donald Miller's Story Brand SB7 Formula.
- A PDF with additional Pillar One content ideas

## Other Free Resources

Our available Free Resources page updates periodically with new free resources such as guides, instructions, templates, and PDFs for in-house employer branding purposes.

Go to https://emine.fi/en/free-resources/.

## *Subscribe to The Magnetic Edge*

Get our exclusive tips, insight, current news, and trends to help you stay ahead of the competition. Subscribe to this free newsletter here: https;//emine.fi/subscribe-magnetic-edge.

## Get Access to Talent Marketing School Online Courses and Masterclasses

Talent Marketing School, our online course platform, gives you access to our employer brand development programs and learning courses designed and taught by Susanna Rantanen. Go to https://talentmarketingschool.com to start your journey to modern employer brand mastery!

Check out masterclasses and learning programs such as:

- Turning Dull Career Stories into Hero Career Stories™
- Instant Employer Brand Accelerator™

# Work with us in Building Your Magnetic Employer Brand

By partnering with us, you can access insights and tools our competitors cannot provide.

**Here's how we help:**

1. Want to have your current employer brand online magnetism audited?
2. Need help creating your Master Plan or aligning your culture with your branding efforts? My team and I offer tailored consulting services to help you implement The Magnetic Employer Branding Method™ with confidence.
3. Employer brand content marketing partnership to implement and execute your content plan each week on social media.

Recruitment marketing on social media, including content creation and paid marketing campaigns. Learn more about our services at https://emine.fi/en.

## *Connect with/Follow Me and Our Agency*

- LinkedIn:
  - https://www.linkedin.com/in/susannarantanen/
  - https://www.linkedin.com/company/employee-experience-agency-emine-oy-ltd/
- Instagram, YouTube, and TikTok: @rantanensusanna
- Instagram: @emineland

# OTHER BOOKS I RECOMMEND FOR YOUR LEARNING JOURNEY

## Employer Branding and Leadership

- *The Culture Code: The Secrets of Highly Successful Groups* by Daniel Coyle
- *The Employer Brand: Bringing the Best of Brand Management to People at Work* by Simon Barrow and Richard Mosley
- *Leaders Eat Last: Why Some Teams Pull Together and Others Don't* by Simon Sinek
- *To Sell Is Human: The Surprising Truth About Moving Others* by Daniel H. Pink
- *Start with Why: How Great Leaders Inspire Everyone to Take Action* by Simon Sinek
- *Drive: The Surprising Truth About What Motivates Us* by Daniel H. Pink
- *Work Rules!: Insights from Inside Google That Will Transform How You Live and Lead* by Laszlo Bock
- *Radical Candor: Be a Kick-Ass Boss Without Losing Your Humanity* by Kim Scott

- *Multipliers: How the Best Leaders Make Everyone Smarter* by Liz Wiseman
- *Employees First, Customers Second: Turning Conventional Management Upside Down* by Vineet Nayar

## Storytelling

- *Building a StoryBrand: Clarify Your Message So Customers Will Listen* by Donald Miller
- *The Science of Storytelling: Why Stories Make Us Human and How to Tell Them Better* by Will Storr
- *Made to Stick: Why Some Ideas Survive and Others Die* by Chip Heath and Dan Heath
- *Stories That Stick: How Storytelling Can Captivate Customers, Influence Audiences, and Transform Your Business* by Kindra Hall
- *Hooked: How to Build Habit-Forming Products* by Nir Eyal

## Marketing and Branding

- *This Is Marketing: You Can't Be Seen Until You Learn to See* by Seth Godin
- *Day Trading Attention* by Gary Vaynerchuk
- *They Ask, You Answer: A Revolutionary Approach to Inbound Sales, Content Marketing, and Today's Digital Consumer* by Marcus Sheridan

- *Inbound PR: The PR Agency's Manual to Transforming Your Business with Inbound* by Iliyana Stareva

- *Youtility: Why Smart Marketing Is about Help, Not Hype* by Jay Baer

- *The New Rules of Marketing and PR: How to Use Content Marketing, Podcasting, Social Media, AI, Live Video, and Newsjacking to Reach Buyers Directly* by David Meerman Scott

- *Contagious: How to Build Word of Mouth in the Digital Age* by Jonah Berger

- *Purple Cow: Transform Your Business by Being Remarkable* by Seth Godin

- *Pre-Suasion: A Revolutionary Way to Influence and Persuade* by Robert Cialdini

- *Hacking Growth: How Today's Fastest-Growing Companies Drive Breakout Success* by Sean Ellis and Morgan Brown

- *Building Online Communities: Branding, Membership, and Social Networking* by Tharwat El-Sakran and others

- *Epic Content Marketing: How to Tell a Different Story, Break Through the Clutter, and Win More Customers by Marketing Less* by Joe Pulizzi

## Organizational Culture

- *The Advantage: Why Organizational Health Trumps Everything Else in Business* by Patrick Lencioni
- *No Rules Rules: Netflix and the Culture of Reinvention* by Reed Hastings and Erin Meyer
- *Rework* by Jason Fried and David Heinemeier Hansson

## Customer and Employee Experience

- *The Experience Economy: Competing for Customer Time, Attention, and Money* by B. Joseph Pine II and James H. Gilmore
- *Delivering Happiness: A Path to Profits, Passion, and Purpose* by Tony Hsieh

# SOURCES, REFERENCES, AND RESOURCES

........................................................................

## Introduction | Business Storytelling to Match Minds with Mission

- Quote by Gary Vaynerchuk: https://www.inspiringquotes.us/ author/1491-gary-vaynerchuk/about-storytelling.
- Citations from neuroeconomist Dr. Paul J. Zak: https://greatergood.berkeley.edu/article/item/ how_stories_change_brain.

## Chapter 1

- Quote by Frances Frei: https://youtu.be/ pVeq-0dIqpk?si=09bMy-DIGtU6tdwk.
- Research by Deloitte: https://www2.deloitte.com/ us/en/insights/focus/human-capital-trends/2015/ employee-engagement-culture-human-capital- trends-2015.html.

## Chapter 2

- Competing Values Framework: https://www.quinnassociation.com/en/robert_e_quinns_competing_values_framework.
- McKinsey & Company's 2020 report titled "Diversity Wins: How Inclusion Matters," www.mckinsey.com.
- PwC's Findings on Organizational Culture and Job Satisfaction: PwC's Global Workforce Hopes and Fears Survey 2022, https://www.pwc.com/gx/en/issues/workforce/hopes-and-fears-2022.
- Gallup's Data on Disengaged Employees and Global Productivity Loss: Gallup's 2024 State of the Global Workplace Report: https://harkn.com/blog/key-findings-from-gallup-s-2024-state-of-the-global-workplace-report/.

## Chapter 3

- Quote by Tony Hsieh: *Delivering Happiness: A Path to Profits, Passion, and Purpose*; Business Plus, 2010.
- Gallup's Data on Disengaged Employees and Global Productivity Loss: Gallup's 2024 State of the Global Workplace Report: https://harkn.com/blog/key-findings-from-gallup-s-2024-state-of-the-global-workplace-report/.

## Chapter 4

- Quote by Donald Miller: *source unknown.*
- Transformative Mission Statement by Donald Miller: *Business Made Simple: 60 Days to Master Leadership, Sales, Marketing, Execution, Management, Personal Productivity and More*; HarperCollins Leadership, 2021.

## Chapter 5

- Quote by Seth Godin: https://seths.blog/2021/12/the-pyramid-of-modern-marketing/.

## Chapter 6

- Talent Persona template, see Resources.

## Chapter 7

- Quote by Arianna Huffington: https://www.greatplacetowork.com/resources/blog/why-arianna-huffington-wants-us-to-stop-saying-%E2%80%98work-life-balance%E2%80%99.

## Chapter 8

- Quote by Seth Godin: https://seths.blog/2009/12/define-brand/.
- George A. Miller: https://link.springer.com/referenceworkentry/10.1007/978-3-540-29678-2_5386.

- https://www.simplypsychology.org/short-term-memory.html.
- Miller, G. A. (1956). "The magical number seven, plus or minus two: Some limits on our capacity for processing information." *Psychological Review*, 63.

## Chapter 9

- Quote by Jeff Bezos: https://www.entrepreneur.com/leadership/what-jeff-bezos-smart-take-on-personal-branding-can-teach/379920.

## Chapter 10

- Quote by Professor Robert B. Cialdini: *Influence: The Psychology of Persuasion*; Harper Business, 1984 and 2006.
- About LinkedIn algorithm changes in October 2023: Talent Marketing School: https://talentmarketingschool.com/kurssit/accelerating-employer-branding-on-linkedin-instagram/.
- Neuroeconomist Dr. Paul J. Zak on persuasive communication: https://youtu.be/IrbrLRQoXBQ?si=H-VGagzEAySH8fg9.
- Donald Miller: Business Made Simple University: https://businessmadesimple.com/.
- Phrase: "Convince and Convert" by author Jay Baer: https://www.convinceandconvert.com/.
- Donald Miller: "The three key characteristics of great communicators": https://youtu.be/ZlJHS2GdG3g?si=CrRh127dEyaNP5db.

- Getting your talent marketing key messages right: https://modernemployerbrand.com/podcast82-getting-your-talent-marketing-key-message-right/.
- Daniel H. Pink: *To Sell is Human: The Surprising Truth About Moving Others*; Riverhead Books, 2012.
- Professor Robert B. Cialdini: "The 6 principles of persuasion": https://www.apa.org/news/podcasts/speaking-of-psychology/persuasion.
- Corporate Employer Brand Influencers: https://www.modernemployerbrand.com/podcast144.

## Chapter 11

- Quote by Simon Sinek and other references to his book: *Start with Why: How Great Leaders Inspire Everyone to Take Action*; Portfolio (an imprint of Penguin Random House), 2009.

## Chapter 12

- Quote by Seth Godin: https://youtu.be/RZ-i3A4_6HE?si=59umCXZrL4xXpgPP
- Lisa Cron: *Story Genius: How to Use Brain Science to Go Beyond Outlining and Write a Riveting Novel (Before You Waste Three Years Writing 327 Pages That Go Nowhere)*; Ten Speed Press, 2016.
- Jeff Hawkins: *A Thousand Brains: A New Theory of Intelligence*; Basic Books, 2021.
- Reaktor, a global tech company: https://www.reaktor.com.

- Christine Comaford: *SmartTribes: How Teams Become Brilliant Together*; Portfolio, 2013.
- Gabrielle Dolan: *Stories for Work: The Essential Guide to Business Storytelling*; Wiley, 2017.
- Donald Miller's StoryBrand Formula (SB7): https://youtu.be/FkCMhhJaSSk?si=Ns413zM9yPsamUkL.
- Joseph Campbell: *The Hero's Journey: Joseph Campbell on His Life and Work*; New World Library, 2003.

## Chapter 13

- Quote by Peter Drucker: *Management: Tasks, Responsibilities, Practices*; HarperBusiness, 1993.

## Chapter 14

- Quote by Robert McKee: *Story: Substance, Structure, Style, and the Principles of Screenwriting*; ReganBooks, 1997.

## Chapter 15

- Quote by Simon Sinek: *Start with Why: How Great Leaders Inspire Everyone to Take Action*: https://simonsinek.com/books/start-with-why/.
- Another quote by Simon Sinek in the post example: *Leaders Eat Last: Why Some Teams Pull Together and Others Don't*; Portfolio, 2014.

## Chapter 16

- Quote by Sheryl Sandberg: *Lean In: Women, Work, and the Will to Lead*; Knopf, 2013.

## Chapter 17

- Quote by Betty Bender: https://blog.zenhr.com/en/2022/01/06/6-inspiring-hr-quotes-to-kick-off-2022.

## Chapter 18

- Widely attributed quote by Abraham Lincoln: *Source unknown.*

## Chapter 19

- Quote by Mary Walton: *The Deming Management Method*; Perigee Books, 1988.

## Chapter 20

- Quote by Rory Vaden: *Take the Stairs: 7 Steps to Achieving True Success*; Perigee Books, 2012.

## Conclusion

- Quote by Gary Vaynerchuk: https://www.convinceandconvert.com/podcasts/episodes/gary-vaynerchuk-and-the-currency-of-attention/.